A Canterbury Tale

A Canterbury Tale

EXPERIENCES AND REFLECTIONS:
1916–1976

John Cogley

A Crossroad Book
THE SEABURY PRESS, NEW YORK

The Seabury Press
815 Second Avenue
New York, N.Y. 10017

Printed in the United States of America

Library of Congress Cataloging in Publication Data

Cogley, John.   A Canterbury tale.

"A Crossroad book."
1. Cogley, John.   2. Journalists—United States—Correspondence,
reminiscences, etc   3. Press, Catholic—United States.   I. Title.
PN4874.C63A32   070.4'092'4 [B]   76-21864   ISBN 0-8164-
0322-8

To the two Churches in my life:

The Roman Catholic Church, which first imparted to me the Christian vision of faith, hope, and charity;
The Episcopal Church, where that faith was purified, that hope strengthened, and that charity, perhaps, expanded.

Contents

	Preface	ix
I.	The Catholic Worker	1
II.	Mott Street	16
III.	Blue Island Avenue	23
IV.	On My Own	36
V.	Commonweal	44
VI.	Blacklist Report	54
VII.	Basic Issues	65
VIII.	Santa Barbara	76
IX.	The Kennedy Campaign	83
X.	Rome	90
XI.	The New York Times	103
XII.	The Center Again	110
XIII.	The Episcopal Church	122
	L'Envoi	126

A selection of photographs follows page 64

Preface

Now that this memoir is completed, I find that I have left out much, including especially my own sins of mind and flesh. I trust that these have been absolved through God's grace and have been consigned to oblivion.

I also discover that I have not done justice to those who have been closest to me throughout the years. Some of these persons are not even mentioned; others enter the narrative only as shadowy actors in the events that led me from one Christian body to another.

I did not really intend this book to be an autobiography in the strict sense. If I had, there are persons I would have had to discuss at length to depict the full story of my life; notably, my wife Theodora; my six children and their spouses; and a host of relatives, friends, and acquaintances. I hope, then, that any seeming slight to those near and dear to me is not misunderstood.

I have been fortunate in the number of other persons, of all faiths and none, and of every race and nationality, who have enriched my life. This would seem to be an appropriate time to thank them for their kindnesses. Perhaps it will suffice to assure them here that their love was returned in full—usually undemonstratively.

One last thought: I may have written harshly of my long years in the Roman Catholic Church. If so, it is because my pen lamentably failed my intention. I have found my best friends and supporters in that communion. I will always be grateful to it, mainly because I was among the millions who inherited the Gospel message from within its fold. Let me, then, express my hope that the Church of my birth and the Church of my adoption will soon enter into full Christian communion. *Ut mox unum sint.*

A Canterbury Tale

CHAPTER I

The Catholic Worker

THIS is a memoir written by a practicing Episcopalian, but it is mostly concerned with the Roman Catholic community in the United States. That is where I spent my life until I was well into middle age.

In his book on the history of *Commonweal**, Rodger Van Allen says that, for a time in the fifties and sixties, I was sometimes called the "pope of *Commonweal* Catholics." I was certainly not conscious of playing this pontifical role, maybe because at the time my relations with the official Church were actually minimal. Writing a column in the pages of *Commonweal* for more than a decade, as I did, was often like talking into a dead mike: there was no response. During my years at the magazine, *Commonweal* was largely ignored by the clergy— neither wooed nor openly denounced.

We did not often have clerical visitors, and most of them were either from the mid-western United States, were European contributors, or were numbered among the suspect priests—like Pierre Teilhard de Chardin, known to us merely as a scholarly Jesuit who wrote incomprehensible books about paleontology. Even Teilhard's visits were few and far between. They were provoked, I now think, by Gallic wonder that in the super-orthodox realm of Cardinal Spellman, an independent organ of Catholic opinion could even

---

*Rodger Van Allen, *The Commonweal and American Catholicism* (Philadephia: Fortress Press, 1974).

1

exist. We rarely met any of the local priests; most of them carefully kept us at arm's length.

There were, in fact, only a few major run-ins with members of the clergy. Once I wrote a piece questioning the "error-has-no-rights proposition," then the official Roman Catholic teaching about church-state relations. I suggested, rather, that the American system of religious freedom was universally applicable and could be squared with Catholic ecclesiology. After the article reached the readers, there was a telegram from a priest-editor (who was later named an official of the Roman Curia) threatening me with an ecclesiastical trial for heresy. To be sure, the position I took was not counseled by seminary texts or the statements of recent popes. It was, however, close to the one later endorsed by the Second Vatican Council. I ignored the threat in the priest's telegram and nothing happened.

Another incident concerned a journalistic award to be given during a student banquet at La Salle College in Philadelphia. The students had chosen to honor me with the award and therefore, I was invited by a teaching Brother to come to Philadephia to receive it. A few days later he wrote again, this time full of embarrassment and apology, to tell me that the award had been cancelled. The diocesan authorities decided that I had been a poor choice, so the Christian Brothers cancelled the whole affair. The students obeyed wordlessly. At the time, my own sense of chancery-office privilege was such that I neither said nor wrote a word about the incident.

Two or three years later, I was invited to address a group in San Diego and, along with Father John Courtney Murray the learned Jesuit, Father Godfrey Diekmann, the brilliant Benedictine liturgist, and a few other speakers, I was blackballed by the late Bishop Buddy of the Diocese of San Diego.

This highly publicized affair led to a fairly footless correspondence between Bishop Buddy and myself. The Bishop had explained to the press that his reason for the action was that he knew one of the proposed speakers in the group was a crypto-communist, who of course would misuse the opportunity to address a group of Catholics.

He would not name the supposed communist, therefore it might have been any one of us. He assured me privately that I was not the one he had in mind, but Christian charity sealed his lips as to who the real culprit was. The affair blew over in time. It was the first case of its kind, in my memory, to receive unfavorable national publicity in the Catholic press.

About this time the pastor of our church on Long Island, a feisty, middle-aged man much given to public temper tantrums, walked to the pulpit one Sunday loaded down with Latin tomes, which he superciliously assured the suburban congregation would be incomprehensible to them if he, with his Brooklyn seminary education, were not there to translate for them. His sermon was instructive; he preached on what he called the "Catholic chain of command." The Trinity accounted for three of the persons in charge. To carry on from there, there were three earthlings—one, the pope of Rome; two, the bishop of the diocese; and three, the preacher himself. Apparently all there was to the life of faith was obedience. Those who followed orders would know what to do and to believe, and they would be eternally saved. Those who had ideas of their own were taking unnecessary risks for the next life.

This sort of thing naturally disturbed me. As relief, I occasionally went to the Cathedral of the Incarnation in nearby Garden City. There, the Episcopal services were carefully and beautifully conducted. The sermons were not always eloquent, but were invariably intelligent. I thought it was a great pity that the Anglican orders were invalid—according to Leo XIII—and that the Cathedral's liturgical actions were therefore meaningless. Otherwise, I should then and there have become an Episcopalian rather than face the ordeal that awaited me every week in my local Roman parish.

I don't want to exaggerate my religious interests. I took no part at all, for instance, in parochial activities or ecclesiastical organizations. But from high school days on, I took more than ordinary interest in abstract theological matters. I accidentally fell into religiously oriented employment, but my real work—whatever it was—was essentially secular.

When I was twenty years old and the country had grown accustomed to the Great Depression, I began to be known publicly (but inauspiciously) as a Roman Catholic. I had already held a series of short-lived, ineffectual jobs: delivering packages for a Chicago department store; working nights in a large, impersonal factory; waiting on customers at a local drug store (where I made delicious ice cream confections and worried about the morality of selling contraceptives); delivering heavy Chicago telephone books to fourth-floor walk-ups; tutoring a high school boy in Latin; and picketing professionally for a dubious union of garagemen. I didn't know what I really wanted to be and, as I consider it now, I was waiting to see what life had to offer.

It seems to me that I found a vocation in journalism and public affairs without deliberately choosing it.

After grade school, I had won a scholarship to St. Philip High School in Chicago, run by the Servite Fathers, a small order of friars founded in 1233. By the time I came along, the Servites' biggest parish was Our Lady of Sorrows, one of the busiest in Chicago. Their high school was next door to the big church. Most of the priests in the large friary attached to it were, like myself, Irish-American Chicagoans. They themselves were usually quite up-to-date, but the order was highly baroque in its liturgical usages, pious practices, and preachments. The special behavior of the order—its particular devotions—were extremely sentimental: they were focused on devotion to the sorrows of the Mother of Christ.

In those days, among Roman Catholics, the word "vocation" meant only the religious life or the priesthood. As a teen-age boy, I was attracted right away to the order. So much so that I fully intended to enter it when I was old enough and to do what I was told by superiors for the rest of a celibate life.

For my second year of high school, I asked to take the special course at a preparatory school located on the outskirts of Chicago, where those who intended to enter the order later were segregated from other St. Philip students. I was accepted, to my delight, and spent the remaining three years of high school in small classes with, surprisingly, only the ordinary religious study requirements (two classes a week on Father Conway's ultra-defensive *Question Box*). There were, however, daily meditations, Mass, endless prayers, and numerous devotions, plus plenty of athletics for sexual sublimation.

Our classes, being smaller, were more intense than the regular courses at St. Philip (though we finally received the same diploma). The years went by slowly; students came and went. We did not think it strange at all that we lived nine months a year under incredible discipline.

Of course we were totally without female companionship. Sex was rarely mentioned among the students themselves, even in their unobserved gatherings. Nor was there any ranting about it by the priests. It was simply ignored. Later I read that Roman Catholic clergy talked endlessly to adolescents about the moral dangers of their sexuality, but I experienced none of that. Perhaps the Italian roots of the Servites overcame the native Irish puritanism of the Fathers.

For reasons I still have not quite understood (though I am sure that sex was a motivating force), I decided one day against being a member of the order and against beginning seminary studies for the priesthood. After I got home, I immediately concluded that I had made a big mistake in breaking ties with the order. But there was no way I could pick up where I had left off. The rules were strict about that. I have never lost my interest in the Servites and still have good friends among them. That vast church on the west side of Chicago is now practically empty on Sunday. St. Philip High School and the preparatory school are no more, and most of the Servite Fathers are dedicated to teaching or to parish work, after the manner of diocesan priests.

At the time I decided against joining the order, I was staying with my grandmother, who had lived in middle class comfort most of her life and was now going through hard times. She owned a modest home on the northwest side of the city but had heavily mortgaged it in a fruitless effort to save her youngest son's business. I came home just about the time she was forced to turn over the property to new owners. My grandmother, with her widowed son and unmarried daughter, was going to move in with another daughter whose husband, a Chicago policeman, was already overburdened. Of course I was included in the arrangement, but my aunt and uncle were so short of space that I would have to share a bed with one of my young cousins.

There was no money for college, though I was eager to enroll in one, and it was assumed that I would go to work and help support the ménage. I found occasional jobs during the months ahead, and I earned enough money to enroll in two courses at Loyola University. In addition, I took the free evening courses in philosophy offered by Sister Thomas Aquinas at Rosary College in nearby River Forest and an unaccredited college course at Oak Park's Fenwick High School. Through these courses and their Dominican professors, I was introduced to the complexities of Thomistic metaphysics.

My special companion was Tom Sullivan, who had been a high school classmate. Tom had a regular job, which made him seem enormously affluent. He was free with his money on our weekends together, and we saw many movies at the downtown first-run houses between endless strolls throughout Chicago.

On one of our city tours, we went into the Franciscan church downtown and found a stray copy of the *Catholic Worker*, which was then in its fourth year of existence. I took it home and was startled by the down-to-earth writing and Ade Bethune's simple woodcuts scattered throughout its eight pages. Bethune's work had life and strength. The saints she delighted in depicting were always employed sweeping floors or mending pots, not simply standing around in spiritual idleness and beatitude. I was used to static, French-inspired religious "art" and, in the more modern centers, the new-style tapered bodies that turned biblical characters into World's Fair mannequins.

A few months after my return from the Servites, my grandmother, the only relative who was unequivocally devoted to my interests (my own mother had died at my birth), suffered a fatal heart attack. I was then on my own and had to sink or swim with no more than a kindly interest on the part of my paternal relatives (maternal relatives were never in my life) who had growing families of their own to support in difficult times.

Chicago was vast and impersonal but, as I discovered on my walks with Tom Sullivan, it contained numerous ethnic neighborhoods with the friendly quality of European villages. It never actually occurred to me that my life might be spent outside the great metropolis beside Lake Michigan. Though I was not very ambitious, I was too "middle class" to take advantage of the assistance the New Deal was offering impoverished youth and too poor not to be concerned about surviving. I continued, then, with the old routines, living temporarily with my oldest aunt and taking back-breaking jobs when they showed up, which was not very often in those days. Generally, my days were spent sleeping or sitting around my aunt's apartment, reading *Anthony Adverse* and other best sellers of the time, and talking with my aunt about the Cogley family.

I also spent a great deal of time in the public library. I was an avid encyclopaedia reader; one article would always lead to another. It was not intended to be a self-educating process, but years later, when I heard Robert M. Hutchins talk about the uses to which the *Encyclopaedia Britannica* might be put, I realized that that's what it was.

I did not really know what to do with my life, and no one else seemed to care particularly. My father was married a second time, had another family, and treated me as if I were a remote leftover from his youth, best forgotten. Though he worked for the city and earned a princely income by our standards, he took no financial responsibility for me. We were on stiffly cordial terms when we met, which was not often. Our relationship was not warm enough to even ignite anger. Occasionaly we went out to dinner and to a movie together but, before these evenings were over, we usually ran out of conversation.

We could not have been more different from each other. I was interested in exploring long-range ideas; he was completely captured by the immediate. I was insecure and initially shy; he was bursting with self-confidence and as friendly as a puppy. I was always questioning. He, on the contrary, never seemed to doubt that he was a member of a latter-day chosen people—being Irish-American—and that he lived in the best part of the best city in the greatest country in the world. If questioned, his loyalty to the Roman Catholic Church would come through, but neither he nor his second wife made any pretense of attending Sunday Mass and they ignored the Church's official fasts and abstinences. They were indifferent to Catholicism, not even bothering to ecclesiastically rectify their city-hall marriage, as far as I knew.

Despite his own indifference, however, my father was the very soul of religious tolerance. He respected my theological proclivities while never particularly encouraging them. He really believed the clichés of the time which I, from a lofty theological height, was always ready to argue about. For instance, he held that one religion was as good as another and that their rituals were all valuable for the crucial times in life, such as birth and death. I took the view that the Roman Catholic Church alone held the keys to salvation and that advocates of other faiths who meant well might indeed be saved, but by their ignorance rather than their wisdom.

I can't say that I ever heroized my father, but I never despised him either. He simply did not count for very much in my conscious life.

I spent a great deal of my endless free time and almost every weekend with Tom Sullivan. We were both ardent movie fans. Nowadays, I sometime see on television the films that held us in thrall, with stars like Clark Cable, William Powell, Myrna Loy, Joan Crawford, Carole Lombard, and of course Greta Garbo.

I suppose one would say that we were "religious" young men. Certainly we obeyed the Church's disciplinary laws, though we were somewhat contemptuous of the peasant piety that existed throughout the archdiocese. We avoided novenas and such special services as May devotions in honor of the Blessed Virgin Mary. If it had not been for the *Catholic Worker*, I would probably have drifted from the Church.

Roman Catholicism, as I see it now, gave an elegant stance of nonconformity to a young Irish-American with neither patrimony nor wealth to strengthen his position. I could always act as if I held the cultural treasures of the Church's long past as my own private heritage. I saw to it that nothing shocked me or was able to dethrone my abstract, peopleless Church. If priests, bishops, or even popes were not all they should have been, so much the worse for them; but not for the Church. It was the Church, wasn't it, that told me what their standards should have been?

I now see that the young, idealistic secularists and humanists were the sounder realists. They took a "by their fruits" view of life and insisted that every philosophy should be judged by its pragmatic result. It was not thus with Roman Catholics. We were preoccupied with "objectivity" and our cultural and theological version of *ex opere operato*, which meant that we could always avoid the answer to "How well does it work?" or even "Does it work?" before switching the argument to purely essentialist terms. As a result, we had a strong advantage in every argument. I know that I often won disputes with persons more burdened with facts and experience than I.

All this changed somewhat when it was announced in the *Catholic Worker* that a group had been organized on the west side of Chicago at the instigation of Arthur G. Falls, M.D. Any Chicagoans who were interested were invited to attend a meeting in a Taylor Street store-front near the Cook County Hospital. I suggested to Tom that we go, and he agreed. Though I did not realize it, we had actually opened the door to a new world. I had already passed my twentieth birthday at this time.

On a Sunday afternoon Tom and I, with no little trepidation, set off for the meeting. Even then, that neighborhood (which has since been leveled to make room for the Chicago campus of the University of Illinois) had seen its best days. It was near Holy Family Church, the big Jesuit parish that forty years earlier had been the citadel of faith for the Chicago Irish. By 1937 the dark, old church was almost empty, even on Sundays. Close by, the Claretian Fathers had a church for Mexicans and the Jesuits also ran a little mission for the few black Catholics in the area. The Holy Family clergy still discouraged their black neighbors from attending the big half-empty church on Roosevelt Road.

We were surprised to learn, then, that the chairman at the incipient Catholic Worker house, Dr. Falls, was a black man. It was unheard of that black people should have positions of leadership in a general Roman Catholic undertaking.

Dr. Falls was more than a decade older than we were and remarkably sophisticated, almost patronizing to his inferiors. His attitude was the opposite of the subservience which the few black people we had known affected for white people. He was a Roman Catholic; not a recent convert, as one might conjecture, but the scion of an old New

Orleans family that had produced a number of pioneering priests and nuns.

The others who showed up for the meeting were all white but, nonetheless, differed greatly from each other. A number of young persons were near our own age. There was Alex Reser, a young man who did routine clerical work for one of the railroads. He was the leader of a group of German-American workers, several of whom accompanied him. The group had become interested in social and intellectual matters by jointly purchasing the "five-foot shelf" set of literary classics. They met in each other's homes regularly to discuss what they had read.

Some other youths were college students. There was Edward Marciniak, a sophomore at Loyola, and Virginia Brady, a freshman at Mundelein College who had come under the influence of a high school teacher, Sister Cecilia, a convert nun who has since celebrated her sixtieth anniversary as a Benedictine.

Sister Cecilia herself and her inevitable companion sister were the only nuns present. The clergy was represented by Father John Hayes, then of St. Angela's parish, who was in his early thirties at the time, and Father Carrabine, a Jesuit youth director who was already past forty.

There other older people present, veteran leaders of the German Catholic social movement, for instance, as well as a number of middle-aged men and women of the kind one might find at almost any parish gathering. Among the latter was the elegantly dressed, witty, sharp-tongued John Bowers, who soon let it be known that he had spent most of the years since the World War in Paris and had quite recently, and reluctantly, returned to the United States. Bowers had no visible means of support, but he subtly suggested an inheritance to explain his obvious prosperity. He was to play an important role in the Catholic Worker movement in Chicago. His very first remark to the group was, "Given a chance, the masses will always make asses of themselves."

The speaker of the day was a strapping young man named Joseph Diggles, a co-worker of Al Reser's. Diggles was a recent college graduate who was at first disappointed that his classical Jesuit education had not prepared him for more than a poorly paying clerical position. Then he learned that he had plenty of time to read on the job, and that made up for it. He was, he said, both a good Catholic and a dues-paying member of the Communist Party. Such an admission, it was clear, was intended to shock the rest of us. It did, especially the *Central Verein* veterans, who argued persuasively that such a dual membership was philosophically absurd. However, the young speaker would not budge from his position.

After the formal talk, we socialized over coffee in the storefront headquarters, agreeing to meet the next Sunday when the speaker would be a Detroit auto worker who had just returned from Russia where he had been employed on an assembly line. His name was Walter Reuther.

For a few months this kind of open-forum presentation continued uneventfully. One of the speakers was Virgil Michel, the distinguished Benedictine liturgist from St. John's Abbey, soon to die. Most of the others were eminently forgettable. There was little or no emphasis on the themes of the *Catholic Worker* itself.

After a while John Bowers, who played more and more of a leading role in the affairs of the group, moved in permanently, sleeping in the rear of what was by now called Holy Rood House. The rest of us were assigned to committees. It finally turned out that we were running a kind of conference center, with religious overtones—we recited Compline together. Soon it became a place that sponsored forums or committee meetings five nights a week.

During the day the ever elegant John Bowers conducted an after-school program for the neighborhood children and spread his influence throughout the largely black community. Once a week he indulged in one of his favorite pastimes—cooking the excellent food available in the nearby ethnic stores. This simply meant that after dinner Bowers enjoyed another of his hobbies—reading from Maritain aloud to a captive but uncomprehending audience who enjoyed the meal and who, after eating, were required to discuss what had been read to them.

These Maritain suppers became well known throughout the city. One time a group of professors from the University of Chicago (which was undergoing a spell of Thomism at the time) came. Bowers was annoyed by their presence and insisted to the regulars that the professors had come for no other reason than to get a cheap home-cooked meal. He went ahead with the reading as usual and then announced, peremptorily, that there would be no discussion that evening because he had a headache and no one present could really take his place in a discussion of such recondite matters. The professors, who had come only for the discussion, left immediately and unceremoniously. Bowers' headache then passed and he carried on as he did every week, allowing for very little or no disagreement.

During this period I was living either with my aunt and uncle or, after I clearly wore out my welcome with them, at the downtown YMCA hotel in a tiny room which cost me three dollars a week. I found it hard to get even that much together and to eat, too. But somehow, with odd jobs here and there and a bit of familial charity, I survived. I spent a great deal of time at the Catholic Worker head-quarters as well.

Some time that spring Dorothy Day came to Chicago. It was the first time any of us had ever met the founder of the Catholic Worker movement. John Bowers claimed that he had known her years before, but his physical description was so far off base that we recognized immediately that he was merely bragging.

Miss Day's visit to the city caused something of a furor when she revealed in her column that she was staying at a rectory in the black ghetto. Women, it seems, were strictly forbidden to be overnight guests in a priest's house. Naïvely enough, Miss Day told all in her chatty, diary-like column. She thereby involved the pastor, Father Drescher of the Society of the Divine Word, in a great deal of personal difficulty. A full though somewhat prettied-up account of her visit was published, of course, after she returned to New York.

In Chicago, there was another story. She was obviously not happy about the way things were going on Taylor Street. There was nothing very wrong with the program and people did remain interested. But a bit of conventional social work among children, Maritain suppers, and numerous committees among the group were not precisely Dorothy Day's idea of how a Catholic Worker house should function in the second largest city in the nation.

Dorothy Day was then about forty and a strikingly attractive wom-an, not conventionally beautiful perhaps, but handsome and even-featured. She was quietly effective in her constant prodding of young people to achieve greater progress in spiritual development combined with detachment and social concern. She herself had not yet achieved the spiritual authority that marked her later years, though she was well on the way.

Characteristically, she gave all the credit for her remarkable ac-complishment to Peter Maurin, an itinerant French philosopher of sorts who was supposed to be learned in a special, insightful way; a man of genuine Franciscan detachment from material goods, ex-tremely humble in manner. Peter Maurin's intellectual genius was clearly exaggerated, but the description of his other personal characteristics was on the mark. He was obviously uncomfortable in the feigned role of leadership. Unless the questions were abstractly philosophical or sweepingly historical, he would turn helplessly to Dorothy Day for an answer. We had no doubt that she was the real leader of the Catholic Worker movement.

No one seemed to think it odd that a woman should be heading a vigorous social movement in the very male-centered Catholic Church, though there was at the time no self-conscious feminism in our cities. Yet Dorothy Day, Catherine de Hueck of Friendship House, and the women of the Grail Movement were all moving spirits in the burgeoning American Catholic "lay Apostolate," as it was called.

Dorothy Day stayed in Chicago for quite a while. We saw her occasionally on Taylor Street. I recall one memorable evening with Tom Sullivan at a cheap restaurant, when she reconstructed her radical past for us. She told stories about her friendships with Rayna Prohme, Emma Goldman, Eugene O'Neill, John Reed, Carolyn Gordon, and practically every prominent social activist we had ever heard of.

Life in the black ghetto where she was stopping was brutal and ugly. Miss Day had decided that there should be a Catholic Worker house there to supplement the work of St. Elizabeth's parish. Completely without consultation with the Taylor Street group, she paid a few months' rent on a ramshackle apartment near St. Elizabeth's rectory, with no specific purpose in mind. She asked Paul Byrne, a Loyola sophomore, and me to move in and take it over after she returned East.

Paul was a dreamy young man who was so intrigued by the writing of Saint John of the Cross that he wanted to drop his studies and go off to join the Trappists in Iowa. His family—prominent, affluent Roman Catholics—disagreed strongly. They could imagine nothing less wise, though religious vocations to the active orders abounded among them. All they were sure of was that Paul's studies were falling off, that he was preoccupied with the Catholic Worker people, and that he had a new friend named John Cogley, who was probably to blame for his switch from a healthy, normal boy to a youth with no material ambition, a sick attraction to the mystical life, and a chillingly censorious social conscience. The charges were only partially true.

Paul and I saw Dorothy Day to the bus station one evening in May, 1937, for her trip back home. At the last minute, she gave us the key to the new place she had rented and a brief set of instructions. Immediately after the bus left the station, we were to go to the striking steel mills and join the massive picket line there. She had heard that there might soon be violence in South Chicago. It was possible that we would be caught in it. "Just think," she said cheerfully, just as if her words did not strike terror in our young hearts, "you might get killed and the Church would have its first labor martyrs."

We joyfully did as we were told and went straight to the turbulent strike scene. The place was crowded and noisy. There were various socialist and communist young people on the picket line, singing popular revolutionary songs and chanting stirring slogans to the effect that Republic Steel had finally met "The People." It was something of a carnival atmosphere. With picket signs in hand, we were quickly exhilarated, losing our initial fear as we marched back and forth in the line. We joined lustily in the strike songs and spent hours in the cameraderie of the picket line. There was no violence that night at all, though a few days later Chicago policemen killed six of the picketers.

Then, after sandwiches and coffee with the others, we started back to our new home in the unfamiliar neighborhood. Muggings and robberies were not so common in those days and we were without fear walking the streets of the black ghetto in the middle of the night. We were not sure what we were supposed to do, but surely opportunities for service would quickly present themselves. We arrived at the barely furnished apartment and talked about future plans. Finally we fell into an untroubled sleep, exhausted by the events of the greatest day of our lives.

About an hour later there was a great banging at the front door. We were scared. Who, in these surroundings, would be visiting in the early hours of the morning, calling on two strange white youths in a solidly black neighborhood? We soon found out. It was a harmless, elderly black woman. As it turned out, she had just arrived in town, after hitchhiking across several states, with our address in hand. She was related to the former tenants and was as surprised to see us as we were to see her. Of course, we offered her our only bed for the rest of the night and took to the floor ourselves. It seemed quite providential that, though its existence was still unannounced, the apartment inadvertently had served as a "House of Hospitality"—as the Catholic Worker houses came to be called—in its very first hours of operation.

The next day we went to Mass and introduced ourselves to the priests of St. Elizabeth's parish as having been sent by Dorothy Day. The pastor invited us to breakfast at the rectory. St. Elizabeth's was an all-Negro parish. Only the priests and the nuns, who taught in the schools attached to the church, were white. The pastor, Father Drescher, was a veteran missionary who had already spent years in the Philippines. He delighted in crude moralisms and rough-and-ready mantalk. He was, as I remember him, as unracist a person as lived in Chicago. He was the first white man I ever knew who referred to Negroes as blacks, fraternally and without self-consciousness.

The rectory was open to all, and it teemed with life. There was always bread and ham or cheese on the table for unannounced visitors and plenty of lively conversation. The place was a friendly center for the whole parish; laughter could be heard from all corners of the house. It was quite different from the few cold, tomblike rectories I had already seen or was to visit in the years to come. Somehow, under the direction of Father Drescher—superficially, the least appealing man in the world—the house was the center of a happy, cheerful, laughing community.

In such a parish, the Catholic Worker was something of a fifth wheel. We did attempt a summer program for the children, but the Catholic Youth Organization (CYO) had long been active in the parish and we were largely duplicating its work. As the outspoken pastor told me one day, we were fairly useless to the life of the area. We did participate in a few straggly little protest parades which were simply ignored by the city fathers. But aside from that bit of social action, the ghetto experiment would have to be counted a failure.

The rent was paid for the summer months, and when the payments ran out, so did the Catholic Worker. I returned to my dingy room at the YMCA downtown, getting an occasional job to make ends meet. But my life at the time was centered on the group that met at Taylor Street, where John Bowers had unquestionably taken over. In this way, the winter passed.

Two of the young men at Taylor Street, Ed Marciniak and Al Reser, had rented an old Italian bakery on Blue Island Avenue, a few blocks from the Taylor Street place, with an apartment above it (only thirty dollars monthly rent for everything). They hoped to make the beginnings of a House of Hospitality similar to the one Dorothy Day had established in New York. At first, very few people came in, even with an inviting plaster statue of Saint Joseph in the window and a welcome sign on the front door.

One of the first guests had experience as a painter, doing sets for cheap burlesque houses, and he decided to decorate the bare walls with garish, sentimental drawings such as he thought proper for a Catholic institution. He was not much of an artist, and the results were predictably awful. But we were finally in business. Al Reser, who added the Catholic Worker chore to his regular job at the railroad headquarters, was in charge. In the spring, just as the Blue Island Avenue venture was getting started, I decided to go to New York to the Catholic Worker headquarters on Mott Street.

CHAPTER II

Mott Street

NEW YORK was everything I thought it was going to be—humming traffic; a certain characteristic elan among the people which gave them a vitality all their own; confidence among its denizens that, if anything important was happening in the world, it had its greatest reverberations if not its origins in Manhattan. One became the proverbial provincial New Yorker soon enough. Though someone who was born and raised in Chicago could hardly be described as a hick, I was as impressed by New York as any yokel.

The Mott Street House of Hospitality—actually two houses, one on the back of the lot—was impressive, too. It was all that Dorothy Day had said it was in her written reports.

Miss Day was, of course, the undisputed leader of a tightly knit, large "family." There were no salaries, no committees, no constitutional provisions; only an unwritten compact that all would live in harmony and voluntary poverty.

The idealism of the young staff, which was based on Roman Catholic theology, was incredible. If Dorothy Day took care of the practical affairs and raised the money to keep the place going, Peter Maurin was the second most important person on the premises. He was in his sixties at this time and still very vigorous. Dorothy Day was a one-woman public relations organization for him. She credited him with the whole idea of the Catholic Worker Movement and drew from his sweeping propositions (which were, at best, only generally applicable) specific concrete conclusions which were later ascribed to him. "Peter thinks that the coffee is too strong," for instance.

16

The result was that Maurin was generally considered to be something of a prophet, with a flair for practical details, and worthy to walk in the shoes of the great philosophers. Some of the young people listened to him reverently, as if they had in their midst a latter-day Aristotle, a one-man university who lived the life of a genuine Franciscan. Peter's utterances were repeated endlessly. Some of the zealots even memorized them.

He was quite aware of his significance and the awe in which he was held, and he enjoyed it openly, somehow without destroying the practical humility that gave him his reputation as a reincarnation of the medieval Poverello. Maurin was absolutely certain of his own identity—French peasant, Catholic heritage, his growing fame a product of Dorothy Day's instinctive talent for American public relations. His reading was stupendous and continuous. His interest in the practicalities and niceties of life was really nonexistent, and his respect for those who had the qualities he himself lacked, indisputable.

He was flattered to be taken seriously by professors of philosophy, and he delighted in shocking business tycoons with outrageous queries that called their whole careers into question. Most of all he took pleasure in the deference he was paid by the young men and women who were attracted to the Catholic Worker, most of them fresh from bourgeois homes and ivy-covered colleges.

Peter, as he was always called—never Mr. Maurin—carried on his informal indoctrinations late into the night. He replied to all questions in sweeping historical generalizations that had been memorized long ago in a sing-songy, verselike literary structure. His remarks were composed for publication. Often he did not actually answer the questioner and he was always eminently impersonal.

A man who took little or no interest in the private lives of the people around him, he nevertheless extravagantly encouraged youth. There were no heights to which his hopes for the young could not ascend. If X showed political interest, he should then be the governor of his state; if Y liked to act, she should be a Broadway star; if Z was something of a public speaker, he should have his own radio show. In my case, he was remarkably prescient. I was interested in journalism. I should, of course, be an editor of *Commonweal* or, if that failed, of *The New York Times*. I managed to be both in the years ahead.

Peter was an incredible *simplificateur terrible*. For instance, his answer to the evils of factory monotony and social inequity was for the United States to copy those pockets of preindustrialized feudal society that still remained in Europe and that he remembered and read about insistently. His answer to the problems of alcoholism and prostitution was for the alcoholics to marry the prostitutes and both to retire to rural life in order to raise children amid healthy surroundings.

In 1938, the Catholic Worker was so crowded that there were no beds at night for me or Lawrence Heaney, a bright young man without much formal schooling, who had come from Milwaukee to sit at Peter's feet. We walked the streets of New York in the small hours, night after night, without fear. Then we went to early Mass, usually with Dorothy Day, at a church in Chinatown. Finally we slept until about noon in vacated beds which had been used the night before.

Heaney and I found a great deal to talk about on our walks. I was fascinated by the mail the *Worker* received and spent some of the night hours going through the files. Most of the letters were elaborately stated positions on contemporary problems. I remember best the long theological treatises in defense of Franco's anti-communist crusade and the syllogistic arguments marshalled against sit-down strikes written by Jesuit professors.

One of the most controversial issues of the day in Roman Catholic circles was the Spanish Civil War. It was viewed by most Roman Catholics as a crucial struggle between the forces of light, represented by the Rebel armies, and the legions of darkness, represented by the Loyalists. The *Catholic Worker*, of course, took a minority position. When the battles were finally over, with a victorious Franco solidly in power, American Catholic partisanship cooled down considerably. I even lived to see the day when the united hierarchy of Spain apologized for its earlier one-sidedness.

American Catholics were expected to fall in line with the leadership of the Church when the Spanish Civil War was going on. The official ecclesiastical press was, by and large, turned into a propaganda apparatus against the Loyalists. Parochial school children, well indoctrinated, prayed fervently for a Franco victory, as if the very fate of civilization were dependent upon it. The Catholic Church, as a result, began to be regarded by most other Americans as hopelessly aligned with feudal privilege and social reaction. And of course the thousands of priests and nuns who were brutally butchered by the Loyalists only strengthened the Catholic conviction that Christianity was facing one of its historical tests. They could not understand how kindly, churchgoing Protestants and Orthodox failed to grasp that point; it seemed so obvious to them. *Catholic Worker* and a very few other publications refused to be caught up in this war fever. Their reluctance, of course, was looked upon as rank disloyalty or subversion.

As for the sit-down strikes, this was much less complex. For the

Catholic Worker not to support these efforts on the part of organizing workers would be to throw its weight behind the resistent owners. There was simply no question of doing that. According to the *Worker*'s position, behind these strikes were years of exploitation, poverty, and want. In "depriving" the owners of their property so that they could not break the strike, the workers who were involved were merely exalting personal rights over property rights in keeping with good and ancient Catholic instinct. This was much too simple an explanation for the learned professors who wrote, weaving their bloodless syllogisms which gave some kind of form to abstract propositions about the rights of ownership and such abiding claims of use and usufruct.

These two issues symbolized numerous others that were to mark me off as something of a maverick in Catholic circles in the years ahead. I often found myself with an embattled Catholic minority, which consistently grew until finally even the Fathers Berrigan became public heroes during the Vietnam war.

But there was one thing after another through the years that challenged basic loyalty. Fealty to this or that cause was casually identified with loyalty to the Church and to the popular position the Church had taken, with allegiance to Christianity itself. Very early there was Father Charles E. Coughlin, the radio orator. Then, years later, Senator Joseph R. McCarthy, who had much the same message. One also had to be a critic of Catholic censorship and the prohibition of certain books if one were to uphold the best America stood for.

Sometimes, it seemed that Roman Catholicism did represent a kind of anti-American infiltration in this country. But to believe this would be to ignore the millions of Catholics who lived quite peacefully under the stars and stripes and still were utterly convinced that Roman Catholic and American interests, rather than periodically clashing, inevitably coincided. Their children might be praying for a Franco victory, and they might be circulating procensorship petitions, but they considered such matters unrelated to their patriotism. In fact, those Americans who disagreed with them should be the suspect ones.

The fact was that American Catholics for years lived successfully in two disparate worlds and somehow managed to conform personally to both. It took me years to realize that there was a sense in which two separate loyalties could coexist in the same person—though it always seemed to them to be only one consistent loyalty.

Visitors to the House of Hospitality abounded. They ranged all the way from the Italian neighbors of the East Side to professors from Notre Dame; a constant procession of men and women, rich and poor, young and old, notable and humble. You never knew who might show up. For instance, one time two Kennedy boys, Joe and Jack, came calling and were offered a very bad meal.

The daily breadline outside the house was long, stretching a full block. It began to form at the break of day. The men lined up along the curb and the staff served them a simple coffee-and-bread breakfast. We did not know where these hungry men spent the night, but they were waiting patiently for breakfast very early every day.

The distribution of donated clothing went on almost all day. The staff, including Dorothy Day, had first choice. There was a great amount of clerical work, acknowledging contributions and mailing out 100,000 copies of the paper, which, in turn, stimulated a great deal of correspondence.

The family meals were where we all got together, although anyone who was around was invited to join. A more motley group would be hard to invent. An eminent French philosopher or a Brazilian prelate might be seated beside a Bowery alcoholic or a *non compos mentis* woman who was persuaded that the drinking water was poisoned. Conversation was voluble and wide-ranging, often heavily theological in nature, though never oppressively so to me.

I recall a discussion in which the subject was "What would you like to do in eternity?" Peter Maurin said he would like to learn from Thomas Aquinas and to argue with Karl Marx. Dorothy Day said she would like to be a simple wife and mother, charged with the care of an ever-growing family. Other people were more flippant. One man, no longer young, said that he would just like to collect the money he had foolishly lent out in his hour of affluence.

One night a week there was a public forum which, in mild weather, met in the courtyard where it could be heard by the Italian neighbors, who hung out the windows to listen to abstruse discussions led by professors from Fordham and Columbia. They were lively affairs, often marked by long monomaniacal comments by the participants.

We also did our share of social action, joining in picketing the fascist consulates, expressing sympathy with current strikes, and, of course, selling the *Catholic Worker* in front of Macy's or outside St. Patrick's Cathedral. I got out of this latter chore every time I could because I found it embarrassing, but some of the young people clearly enjoyed such an assignment and actually volunteered for it.

So the work went on, and we heard encouraging reports that the

Catholic Worker was growing throughout the country. Each house, of course, was expected to raise its own funds, but all looked to Dorothy Day for leadership and to Mott Street for an example.

A few of the young couples in the movement had set up house-keeping in rural communes. They were desperately poor, but they did not seem to mind. There was much talk about the benefits of the simple life, but not a great deal of farming was actually done. Most of the work was done by experienced men who had originally come seeking a handout.

Poverty was highly regarded at the Catholic Worker houses; none of the young people admitted to any ambition other than being poorer still. Loyalty to the Church, despite the criticism that was then being hurled at the movement by important Catholic priests, was im-pressive. Clericalism was abhorred, to be sure, but members of the clergy were always given a warm, respectful reception and their words were received with more than ordinary attention. There was a great sense of lay freedom—later expressed as "*We* are the Church"—but little serious anti-clericalism.

Dorothy Day held everyone, herself included, to a very high stan-dard of personal morality and religious devotion. Daily Mass and Communion were the norm for the staff. The sexual looseness of some of our radical friends was looked upon as one of their handicaps—like not having a share in the true faith. Tolerance and respect for the beliefs of others was taken for granted and the mildest bigotry was frowned upon, but the movement was indisputably Roman Catholic and very concerned with the personalities and sub-jects then dominant in the Catholic world.

Life was pleasant enough at Mott Street. Amenities were at a minimum, but the two young men who were chiefly responsible for order in the house had high standards of cleanliness and were forever scrubbing and cleaning. The fetid odor of urine hung over the place, though, no matter what they did; but we all got used to that too.

There came the day when I was asked to leave and return to Chicago in order to take over the now thriving house on Blue Island Avenue. It seems that two of the Chicago group, Al Reser and Catherine Ready, were going to get married. They intended to estab-lish a home near the Chicago Catholic Worker, but a replacement was needed at the Blue Island Avenue House of Hospitality. Someone was required to be there all the time to keep things going, Al wrote. The wedding was scheduled for November; I should come back (bus fare was included in the letter) as soon as possible.

My own inclination was to stay where I was, but everyone agreed that I was needed in Chicago, and no one even suggested that I was indispensable at Mott Street. Until the last minute I secretly hoped someone would suggest that I might write for the paper, but no one did. My journalistic calling had not yet been recognized by anyone but Peter Maurin.

Returning to Chicago meant giving up the vitality and youthful comradery of the original house. But I was aware of my duty, and at the last minute I left New York and crossed the eastern United States, ready to assume responsibility for what I actually remembered as a somewhat ill-conceived House of Hospitality.

I had just turned twenty-two.

CHAPTER III

Blue Island Avenue

I GOT back to Chicago before the Ready-Reser wedding and moved into St. Joseph's House of Hospitality. The place was now jammed full. It was the decision of the engaged couple to hold their wedding reception in the Blue Island Avenue house, though the actual marriage would take place at the bride's bourgeois parish church in another part of the city. It was a mixed group gathered around our long tables for the wedding feast: Catherine's highly respectable, middle-class family; Al's working-class relatives; visiting Catholic Worker people from nearby Milwaukee, Cleveland, and St. Louis; the group that had met at the Taylor Street center; the guests in the new Blue Island Avenue house; and, of course—as Al insisted— "the lame, the halt, and the blind" who wandered in off the street for the usual soup.

After the Resers left for a brief honeymoon, I found myself for the first time completely in charge of the Catholic Worker.

In 1948, in an article written for *America*,* I gave an accounting of those days. The following, in part, is what I wrote, taken from personal notebooks kept at the time:

The first day the house on Blue Island Avenue was opened three men showed up and asked to stay. There were still no beds in the place, so they

*From "Store-front Catholicism" by John Cogley. Reprinted with permission from *America*, 1948 All rights reserved © 1948 by America Press, 106 W. 56 Street, New York, N.Y. 10019

23

slept on the floor. More came the next day, and the next, and the next. Within a few weeks there were almost three hundred men sleeping on the floor every night wrapped in newspapers. One of the first donations came from the Poor Clare nuns, who offered twenty-five or thirty cots with hard Franciscan mattresses. The old men slept on these; the young ones found places on the floor, under beds and tables, and even on the wide display counter at the storefront widow. It was a bitter winter in Chicago. After the place was chock full, with men wedged in like cigarettes in a pack, it was heartbreaking to tell another hundred standing outside the door, shivering and pleading, that there was no more room and they they would have to "carry the banner" for the night. Inside, the house was heavy with the stench of unwashed bodies and filthy clothes; noisy with eerie, spoken nightmares and the sudden shouts of troubled sleep.

This is the way things had become while I was still in New York. The place, Al Reser assured me, was in a constant uproar during the day and a frightening scene of human degredation by night.

Authorities from the Health Department came around one day with charts and tapes and measuring sticks. They scrupulously measured the distance from bed to bed and the number of cubic feet in a room. They presented us with their findings and said the house was a disgrace—to the neighborhood, to the city, and to the Catholic Church. Henceforth, we were to limit ourselves to forty men, the maximum number that could live in the place.

We pleaded for the three hundred men we normally housed. "Where are they to go?" we asked. "What about *their* health, sleeping out on the streets, in doorways, and in the rat-infested alleys all night? Aren't you interested in *their* health?"

"Our job is to inspect lodging places," they said. "We can't underwrite the health of every bum in Chicago. Why do you worry about them? They'll get by. Now you keep the rules we made, or we'll close the joint up."

So the selection had to be made, and that night there were almost three hundred shivering outside the door instead of the usual small number of left-overs. We told them what had happened and why the floors were empty that night, and we invited them to come back for breakfast. They took the news with the same grumbling patience with which they received similar blows from all welfare agencies, and disappeared down the side streets and the alleyways.

The next morning they were all at the back door, waiting for oatmeal and coffee. That was the beginning of the breadline which was to continue unabated three times a day until the house was finally closed.

Thousands passed through the place. As in one of those montage sequences in the movies, faces become blurred in memory when you try to associate definite features with the anonymous people in the old notebooks. There were so many men and—because of the crowded conditions—so little quiet that people, days, incidents get jumbled up. But a few stand out, unforgettable for one reason or another.

There is this paragraph among the notes:

I spent all afternoon talking with one of the men in the house when I should have prepared the talk to be given in the evening. I told the audience to pray for him. He is an ex-convict, just recently out after serving twenty years. He was only a boy when he went in. Throughout that long twenty years he received Holy Communion regularly every month. He can't keep a job after his record is discovered. He was plunged deep in despair this afternoon. I promised to get him a job. This neighborhood is bad for him. He should get away from sordid surroundings. After such a life, he has a right to the clean and wholesome.

The whole story isn't in the notebook. I talked that night to a community of priests and seminarians at a Benedictine monastery near Chicago. I told them the story of the ex-con and asked them to pray for him, that he would find employment away from skid row.

Three or four days later, the fellow came in to say that he had gotten a job through an ad in one of the Catholic papers. He was now employed as a gardener and caretaker at the very monastery where I had talked.

"Did you tell the Fathers about your past?" I asked.

"No. They didn't ask about anything, and I figured that what they don't know won't hurt them."

I felt the same way. However, there was a deliciousness about the good monks unwittingly answering their own prayers that was hard to keep secret. Another entry calls forth a definite image:

A boy wandered in to us today, thin and wan, a pinchfaced, round-shouldered, frightened looking kid from Texas. He had run away from home three weeks ago. If his story was true, he had every reason to do so. He spoke of a jealous stepmother and a henpecked, indifferent father. His body was clumsy and he was inarticulate—he was so scared—and it was hard to piece his story together. We discovered him in the breadline this morning. No place for a kid his age—he couldn't be more than fifteen, although he said he was seventeen.

It seems that last night he stopped in at one of the soup-and-salvation missions along State Street. "They was praying and palm-singing and making testimony," he said. When the persons in charge learned that he had no place to go, they offered him the best that they had there. But they kept him up until two o'clock in the morning while four adults circled him, demanding that he be saved and confess his sins. The kid was tired after tramping the roads all day, and he was willing to be saved or anything else if he could only get some sleep. He told them he would confess to anything they wanted.

But they didn't believe his voice was firm enough to denote conviction. While the night wore on, they attempted to bolster his faith with facts, carrying on theological discussions for his benefit. In the morning he was aroused before six and sent over here for breakfast. We sent him to the CYO, where he would be among youngsters his own age. The poor kid did all he could to sound like a Dead Ender, but his voice quivered.

There were many to remember for various reasons. One time a fortyish Irishman, who had long been a family man and wasn't used to the ways of skid row (I remember that he could not for the life of him roll a cigarette), disappeared for a couple of days. He had been so despondent about whatever it was that had happened at home and that led him to skid row, that the others believed that he must have committed suicide. Then his picture appeared in the papers one evening. He had been found wandering downtown without any trousers and could not explain why. The papers treated the story as a big joke. We never saw the man again.

Another time we unknowingly gave hospitality to an escaped Nazi aviator who had dramatically taken leave of a Canadian prison. He stayed at the house three or four days, washing dishes every time the line passed through and jotting down mysterious notes in a little book. He might have passed through the place unremembered except that he never said a word all the while he was there and everyone recalled him as "the Dummy."

Still another dramatic memory is about one of the younger men who listened to a lecture by a priest one night and then came around to talk later. He asked about confession. How far could you trust a priest to keep the seal? I told him there were no limits. Then he told me about a murder he had committed years earlier. He had never been found out. Was I sure the priest wouldn't talk? I insisted that I was surer of the priest than I was of myself. He went to confession.

There was a young alcoholic who had once been in a seminary. One afternoon he came in shivering and weeping and begging for a drink. It was my first experience with the DTs. The big room was full of men who were used to cases like his. The drunk thought he was going to die and kept screaming out "I'm dying! I'm dying!" Then he knelt down beside me and began to make his final confession. "Bless me, Father, for I have sinned. It is ten years . . ." I told him to stop it; that there was no priest there. But he kept it up, naming his sins and crying out his repentance. One by one the men in the room left, embarrassed by the scene. I sat with the stricken man while he repeated over and over "Jesus Mercy! Jesus Mercy!" until the cops came in to take him away to the county hospital. In a few weeks he was back, drunk again.

A nun/professor from one of the Catholic girls' colleges came down every Saturday morning with her students to wash dishes and serve the men in the noon line. One Saturday she brought one of her religious students, a black Oblate Sister. The sight of the two of them, nuns of two orders, of two races, working together in the kitchen, made a deep impression on the men. Somehow it was a more convincing argument than all the pamphlets we distributed and all the learned lectures we sponsored.

Another note about a man who stands out:

> One of the men in the house was stricken with a serious heart attack a few weeks ago, and his life has been hanging on a thread ever since. He is a silent, sullen person who cherishes an unreasonable prejudice against medicine and medicos. He refused to see a doctor. Late one night, giving in, he asked us to call one for him. The doctor told us to send him to the hospital in the morning.
>
> The next morning he was worse. The doctors at the hospital didn't

think he was going to last the rest of the day. So they called us in the afternoon. When we got to the hospital he was being examined and treated; doctors and nurses kept moving silently and seriously in and out of his room. We sat out in the corridor, waiting for word one way or the other. A little Jewish woman shared the bench with us. Her husband was dying, and he was stretched out in the room across from us where she could watch him. He was silent and still, only tossing nervously every half hour or so. At every move she looked to see if he were regaining consciousness. She kept repeating over and over, "It's a hard life. It's a hard life," like some consoling chant.

Our sick man has no faith and was known here at times to declare without qualification that all religion was a racket. He isn't bitter or bigoted; rather, his is a terrifying indifference. It seemed cruel to let him go without any spiritual consolation at all when we realized he was dying. I asked him if he wanted to see a clergyman. Even in his weakness he said, "Certainly not!"

We passed inane, studied remarks to each other, and then he grew gentle and nostalgic, thinking of the sleepy little town in Vermont where he had grown up. He tried to describe his home—the peace of the place and the precious pretensions of the people. But the doctors came in and told him not to talk. As we left he smiled at us. "If it will make you feel better," he said, "I'll see a priest."

If it would make *us* feel better! Here was a kindly rebel, consistent even on his own deathbed. He revolted early against the little town; he was in revolt against the supposed wisdom of doctors and theologians; he was in revolt against the idea of dependence—even on God; and now there was only this sweeping tolerance of another's whims. No sense of being in need, a dry toleration for the weakness of others and their childish dependencies, which were not for him even lying in a pauper's hospital bed, taking his last beating.

The man died. It wasn't until months later, after we were able to trace his folks, that we learned he was the son of a doctor and that his brother was a Christian minister.

I think of two men whenever I hear the gospel about the poor being always with us. Both are in the notes.

One old man here now is a striking person. He is simple and gentle, polite to a fault. He came here to eat for months before we learned that he had no place to live. He wears a straggly beard, which is his great pride.

The old man has a deep desire for security and a craving for personal property, manifested in an untidy, almost anti-social way. He collects things: the leftover copies of *Novena Notes* in the churches he visits, free booklets and street guides, pieces of discarded clothing, and rags he finds in the alleys. They are all precious to him. He is especially fond of his religious booklets and holy pictures, which he pores over studiously.

This strange accumulation is his only property. He watches over it jealously. He never leaves the house without collecting all the junk together and taking it with him. Usually, too, he stacks away a few pieces of bread to munch on during his walks.

Once the old man had a chance at real security. He was established at a home for the aged, but he would not stay. The person in charge insisted that he dispose of his collection. He refused, and came back to the streets rather than part with his leaflets, pamphlets, holy pictures, rags, medals, and broken pieces of discarded costume jewelry.

Here is the note on the second.

One poor old fellow is a real problem. He is simple minded and for years he has wandered around the streets of Chicago with no one to look after him. He should have constant attention. He was just returned after a stay at the county hospital, where he was treated and tapped for dropsy and then dismissed. He lives in a child's world, all alone. Someone has to keep an eye on him all the time. His name is Alex.

A few weeks ago Alex disappeared for two days. He came back, his feet swollen like balloons. It seems he was on his way back here from his wanderings when his legs gave out. He couldn't go any farther and collapsed on the street. Hundreds of people passed by, but they just left him there, probably thinking he was drunk. He begged a policeman to arrest him, but the cop smelled his breath, decided he wasn't drunk, and left him in the alley where he had staggered. He huddled there by a garbage can all night, while the rats danced around him. The next morning he staggered back here, step by step, and fell as he reached the door. We brought him to the county hospital, where he was well treated.

Eventually Alex was committed to a state institution. I found this among the old notes, too:

Rose Lathrop chose as her motto a saying from Saint Vincent de Paul: I am for God and the poor. Men are men, and human nature is what it is, and it is often discouraging. You run into deceit and rank ingratitude. You expect it, of course, and yet it never comes that it doesn't bring disappointment and discouragement. To be for the poor means to be for the outcast and the underdog. You make your interests one with those of men and women without honor. For it is sad but true that poverty here in America suggests shame and disgrace. Men are almost always blamed for their own poverty.

We have a phrase, much used, that speaks well for our general attitude toward the poor—"poor but honest." It's telltale. We know that injustice and exploitation exist, yet when we come in contact with a victim of these sins (for they are sins) we look at him long-sufferingly. Far too willing to tolerate destitution, we become in a niggardly way tolerant of the destitute. It is something to think about—how much of what we consider charity is, in the long run, the barest justice. God knows there is a great need for both.

It became obvious soon enough that to support the house, we were going to have to raise the wherewithal. People were generous. A Mrs. Brennan, widow of a one-time Chicago political boss, contributed the monthly rent. The diocesan seminarians at Mundelein, led by the quiet-spoken young man who would become Monsignor Daniel Cantwell, took up collections for us. The Poor Clare nuns had monthly deliveries of food deposited at the door. The Servites, running their successful Novena to Our Sorrowful Mother, sent us a small monthly contribution. Father Carrabine and his students helped. Bishop O'Brien, the auxiliary bishop of the diocese, visited us unannounced one night, and ended up giving us the offering made to him for the Confirmations he had just conferred.

However, we needed more as the line of men outside our door increased. We decided therefore to broadcast our plight and publish our own *Catholic Worker*. I was named editor of the new publication. Thus did I begin my career as a professional journalist. The periodical, eight pages in length, came out monthly, although our finances were so low that we missed publication from time to time. The *Chicago Catholic Worker* ran for three years.

We were publishing regularly when James O'Gara, who was two years younger than I, joined us as a resident worker. O'Gara was a talented writer and immediately started to contribute to our pages. Years later he was to be editor-in-chief of *Commonweal*.

Of course, our time was given over to the running of the house, but somehow we also fitted in inspirational talks at the local Catholic high schools and colleges, and to other interested groups. Certainly we did not suffer from any lack of female company. Many of the girl students at the local colleges took an interest in our work—and perhaps in us—and often dropped by to see how we were doing. We also ran forums once a week and participated personally in some of the local strikes that were heralding the birth of the Stockyard Workers, the Steel Workers, and the Newspaper Guild.

Our relatives, Jim's and mine, worried about us. They thought we were wasting our youth, but we could not imagine a better way to spend it. There was a great deal of hitchhiking from one Catholic Worker house to the other. Every now and then either Dorothy Day or Peter Maurin would drop by the Blue Island Avenue place. There was, of course, a great deal of traveling around the country on our part as well. There were about forty Catholic Worker groups running houses and communal farms from coast to coast and we occasionally visited them.

I was a big musical comedy fan and thought nothing of hitchhiking from Chicago to New York to see a matinee performance of *Pal Joey* or *Du Barry was a Lady*. I stayed at the Catholic Worker house when I reached Manhattan and then hurried home to my duties in Chicago after the performance, which I had originally read about in *The New Yorker*.

One day when I was out, we had a visitor—a young girl who drove up in her father's Buick. She had been recently graduated from the University of Chicago and lived with her family in Hyde Park. She asked Jay Morgan, who received her, if there was anything she could do to help. She explained that she had been summoned back to Chicago from Greenwich Village by her parents and was finding life at home very dull. A friend in New York had told her to look us up when she returned to Chicago. Morgan said that she should come back when I was there.

When I returned, Jay—one of the younger men who had originally come to us looking for a handout—waxed eloquent about our visitor. He said she was very beautiful, gracious in manner, and bore a striking resemblance to Ingrid Bergman, then a rising young star.

A few days later she returned as promised and, as Jay predicted, I was immediately and hopelessly stricken with Theodora Schmidt, whose last name I thought was dreadfully prosaic for so ravishing a girl. I had very little for her to do but told her to return for secretarial work. There were some thank you notes to be typed, a task that Jim O'Gara or I usually performed ourselves. She returned and did the assigned task. Even then, we did not pair off, but every now and then we joined in the merrymaking of the younger group centered around the Catholic Worker.

We were brought closer together by my interest in the theater. One of our regular visitors was a member of a group called—meaninglessly, but in the spirit of the times—the Catholic Labor Theater. He came in one day to tell me that the group had been chosen to entertain at Father Daniel Lord's Summer School of Catholic Action at the Morrison Hotel, a huge gathering of college students from all over the United States. The Labor Theater had decided on what I regarded as a creaky, ancient melodrama for their performance.

I was indignant. "Why couldn't they do something more modern than this?" I asked. "There are no other plays we can afford," he said, "unless you write one." I agreed then and there to write a play and have it in his hands when the first rehearsal was scheduled. Then there was a halt; I forgot my promise. As the time drew near, my friend began to grow fearful that the promise was only an empty boast, and he told me so. Finally, I realized I had to fulfill my glib vow, though I did not have any idea of what to write about. Certainly my life as it was then did not strike me as a proper subject for the light play that I knew was needed.

I decided I had to get away from Chicago to do it. Where, I did not care. I found I had enough cash for a trip to Dubuque, Iowa, and started out by bus. When I got to Dubuque, one of the first things I saw was a bus with a sign on it: "To Mount Carmel Motherhouse," headquarters of the B.V.M. nuns. Who, I suddenly asked myself, would create the biggest stir by entering a convent? The answer came: a Lana Turner or some other sexy movie star of the highest voltage. I realized that I had my play and couldn't wait to get to the small hotel room I had reserved and to begin *I Wouldn't Want to Live There*.

When I brought it back to Chicago, the Catholic Labor Theater group found it acceptable and was quite willing to produce it. Theodora, among others, tried out for the leading role, which she landed without any trouble. Rehearsals were held throughout the summer, and the author scrupulously attended them. The proximity of the author and the leading lady during this period brought Theodora (who worked as secretary to Saul Alinsky, the social activist) and me much closer together; but there was nothing formal about our relationship.

The play was a success. Its uncritical, unsophisticated audience laughed in the right places, and Father Lord predicted, to my pleasure, that its author would soon be writing for Broadway. The play, I know now, was quite amateurish. It was decided that, with such success, *I Wouldn't Want to Live There* should be given for a week at the Loyola Community Theatre and at a few of the burgeoning military camps in the Chicago area. Again, success. The leading lady was singled out by an MGM scout, but she turned down his offer.

Finally, the war we had hoped to avoid was with us. Dorothy Day and the Catholic Worker were, of course, officially pacifist—dictatorially so for a short spell. Most of the Chicago group, however, were obstinately "interventionists," as we called ourselves. Certainly we produced no trouble for the draft board.

Tom Sullivan and Jim O'Gara were duly drafted; the gentle Jim into the infantry, with which he served in New Guinea, and Tom into the air force. Tom spent most of the war in the South Seas. I might have escaped the draft entirely. It was clear that after three and a half years, the established house would have to be shut down if I went into the service. Without my knowledge, Monsignor Reynold Hillenbrand, then the popular rector of the seminary at Mundelein, wrote as much to the draft board.

I was called before them, and they—almost all Italians who were unduly impressed by a letter from an important monsignor— suggested that I accept a deferment in the "national interest," in order to keep St. Joseph's House going. I had created such a fuss in the Catholic Worker by my "militarism" that I simply had to refuse the board's offer—much to their surprise. Finally, we agreed on a compromise. If they would wait until all the old men still in the house had found new homes, I would be pleased to be drafted. My scruples at the time were such that I could not enlist; to avoid responsibility for killing others, I thought I had to act in obedience to a group of my fellow citizens.

In accordance with my promise, I had to see that the unemployable men in the house were taken care of. The Little Sisters of the Poor who really lived their vocation, eventually took all of them without hesitation. I was free of a responsibility that was certainly a maturing one, but, I realize now, altogether too much so for one of my years and lack of experience. For instance, I am not surprised to remember that I occasionally found myself weeping for no apparent reason. The food was poor, the pangs of hunger frequent, and the burden of having the responsibility for so many older people without hope was sometimes overwhelming.

Theodora and I grew closer. On April 6, 1942, knowing that I would soon be drafted, we were married in the small chapel at St. Thomas the Apostle Church by one of my Servite friends, young Father Gregory O'Brien. After a honeymoon week in New York, we returned to Chicago—Theodora to her job with Alinksy, I to unaccustomed idleness.

The draft board was duly informed that I was now available for military service. A few weeks later, I was inducted and a new chapter opened in my life.

REFLECTION ONE

This period, the Catholic Worker phase of my life, was completed. I never picked it up again, but I have remained on friendly terms with some of the people I met on Blue Island Avenue and Mott Street. Years later, I gave a course in philosophy at the House of Hospitality in New York. Tom Sullivan, who was in charge of the New York house for a full decade after his return from the South Pacific, still keeps in close touch both with Dorothy Day and with me.

The time I was actually involved in the work of the movement was crucial. It was comparatively brief, but I experienced it at a formative age—my early twenties—and it had a tremendous influence on my life and subsequent behavior.

First of all, though I was clearly over my head when I began, I realized later that I had gained a certain practical judgment that may have come ahead of schedule because of the Catholic Worker.

Second, it gave me my first training in journalism. Being responsible for a small monthly, doing everything from writing editorials to making up the pages, inspired a certain self-confidence that enabled me to tackle the editorial jobs that came along later.

These, however, are minor considerations. The main contribution was to my thinking. The movement has recently been highly lauded. During my time with it, it was unreasonably suspect. For instance, in Chicago one of our Jesuit pastors was certain that we were subversive Communists. Others of the clergy dismissed us as simple religious kooks. One well known priest hired a detective bureau to prove that Dorothy Day was hypocritically leading a double life. He got wind of the scandalous affaires d'amour of someone else by the same name and hastily concluded that the lady in question must be the leader of the new movement whose very name sounded foreign to the ambitious middle-class Catholicism of the era. Our Dorothy Day, needless to say, came through the investigation with her reputation unscathed.

I sometimes think that it was only Miss Day's own high standards of personal contact that saved the rest of us, who were young enough to succumb to vapid censoriousness and self-righteousness. Our immediate daily contact with the victims of poverty de-romanticized social involvement. It was difficult for us to put all the blame on social disorders and none on man himself when we were hourly faced with the most unlovely exhibitions of human perversity—lying, cheating, duplicity, drunkenness, drug addiction.

Decades later, I was put off by what I considered to be the affected moral *superiority displayed by the radicals of the sixties. Perhaps my contempt grew out of nothing more substantial than the growing conservatism of the age. I like to think, however, that I first learned to combine my indignation at structural social evil with understanding and compassion for my fellow man at the Catholic Worker.*

I am astonished now at the high ideals we had and how well they were carried out by so many young people—ideals that grew out of the tradition of Roman Catholicism. Protestant, Orthodox, and Jewish supporters and readers were welcome in the Catholic Worker world, but the movement itself was overwhelmingly Roman Catholic. The inspiration for Peter Maurin's utopian schemes to create a new society within the shell of the old was derived en bloc from his religious tradition. Dorothy Day's piety was nurtured by the ideals found in the lives of the saints, somehow marvelously integrated with the noble Marxism she had been exposed to earlier.

We were, of course, very avant garde in our critique of the social order and our disdain for what Miss Day contemptuously called "Holy Mother the State." But our criticism of Holy Mother the Church did not go far beyond an occasional mild dose of anti-clericalism.

We looked upon non-Roman Catholics then as generally admirable and sincere, but tragically misled. We were utterly conventional in our pre-Vatican II ecclesiology: there was only one true Church and, through the grace of God, we knew where to find it. Its members, even its leading clergy, might be no better than they should be, but then, we were quick to point out, neither were we.

The Church laid down the guidelines, whatever the subject. Who were we to challenge our betters? We might disagree, and often did, with the practical interpretation of Catholic social doctrine, but the abstract dogma was beyond argument. And by dogma, I mean not only the basic understanding of the biblical faith but the doctrines developed over the centuries. No one, for instance, questioned the existence of purgatory or the infallibility of the popes. No one questioned indulgences or had any scruples about giving honor to the relics of the saints. The sinfulness of contraception went without saying.

One time, during an interview about the Catholic Worker, Dwight Mac-Donald of The New Yorker *told me that he should have expected Dorothy Day to turn to Quakerism once she had finally settled on Christianity. I disagreed. It seemed to me that the sacramental element in Catholicism fulfilled a psychological need of Miss Day's that the Friends ignored. For instance, she took pleasure in genuflecting, holy water, sacred signs, and bodily movements in worship. She was, however, strongly attracted to the Quakers' pacifism and vigorous social action.*

My own reaction to the rigid orthodoxy of the Catholic Worker was that it actually kept my mind off theology. During those years, I never asked why I was where I was. I took the Roman Catholic faith to be as much a part of me as my own body. I rarely, if ever, let my mind drift into doubt—not only about the basic Christian revelation but about Roman Catholic peculiarities. Doubt could lead to sin and sin could lead to God knows where. Regularly, I dutifully went to confession and received Holy Communion.

In the meantime, I was growing intellectually. For some time, through Father Carrabine's good offices, I took advantage of the scholarship which a young man who was then in the Jesuit novitiate had earned at Loyola. I remember leaving the bedlam of the house in order to attend a Loyola class in Thomistic ontology. No one could guess what I had just left before I gave myself to a discussion of Aristotelian matter and form or substance and accident. I did not tell them. For some reason, I was silent about my lifestyle.

The Catholicism of the Catholic Worker went unquestioned. The young people in the movement have struck their fellow Catholics as too insistent on drawing out the full social implications of the faith, but they were strictly observant and devout. Had I remained in the movement this story might never have been written.

CHAPTER IV

On My Own

MY military service—which went on for as long as my association with the Catholic Worker movement—was thoroughly
undistinguished and undangerous. It would be no exaggeration to
say it was a flop. For all my vigorous anti-Nazism, I did almost
nothing to defeat Hitler. Throughout the war I remained in army air
force stations in the United States—Illinois, Missouri, Florida, New
York, Kentucky, Utah, and California—in utter safety and compara-
tive comfort.

I was chosen, first of all, to be a radio operator. The training completed, I was sent to join a night fighter squadron that was being
assembled in Florida and was destined to enter the European theater.
As was the custom, the air force sent more men than were needed for
the incipient squadron. A few had to be left behind for further assignment. It so happened that at the very hour the choice had to be
made, I received a telegram announcing that Theodora had given
birth to our first child, a red-headed boy. This, of course, tipped the
scales in my favor and I was one of those left behind when the
squadron flew off to North Africa.

From then on, for the next three and a half years, I remained in the
United States. By the time I was released from the service, my twenties were drawing to a close. I was the father of two children, a boy
and a girl—Terence and Ann. I was eager to get on with some kind of
life in the civilian world. Return to the Catholic Worker seemed out of
the question. I had seen too many families undergo unbearable

36

strains due to their attempts to combine the routine of the Worker and family life.

During the war I had corresponded with Jim O'Gara in New Guinea about how we would spend our lives. Inevitably, the project we envisioned was journalistic. Each of us had an additional goal: to complete the college education intermittently carried on since high school, years before.

Jim, suffering from malaria, was home by the time I received my discharge from the service. We got together right away and made plans to organize a new publication. As we had it figured out, it was to be a kind of general version of the *Chicago Catholic Worker*. We thought of it as an up-to-the-minute review of secular affairs as they affected the Catholic community. We had ideas, we were young and optimistic, and we already had some experience. All we needed, it seemed, were the funds to get the venture off the ground.

We set off to Seattle to solicit funds from a wealthy woman, a friend of Father H. A. Reinhold, a sympathetic German refugee priest I had first met on Mott Street.

Our short stay in the state of Washington was an unqualified success. Father Reinhold's friend contributed one thousand dollars to the project on the priest's assurance that we were honest young men, capable of doing the job we had in mind, and brimming with Christian social idealism. The thousand dollars (which it took years to repay) was used for a trip to New York, where we tackled Father Reinhold's *really* rich friends for more funds. In New York, we were admitted to a few elegant offices and smart East Side homes, but it was clear soon enough that this was the wrong set for two young men of very liberal opinion.

We were closely questioned by our supposed benefactors, whose political opinions were very conservative and whose religious orientation was quite different from our own. We kept giving the wrong answers about racist practices, union organizations, and the social effects of our commitments to Roman Catholicism. As a result, we were not terribly surprised to be politely turned away time after time.

Finally, after a number of futile calls at Wall Street offices and swank brownstone drawing rooms, we sadly concluded that the Manhattan venture was a failure.

Back home, I was advised by the admissions officer at the University of Chicago to return to Loyola. Under a new Chicago system, the college credits I had painfully garnered before the war would not be worth a great deal. I went back to Loyola not quite a junior. There was no tuition problem this time, since education was covered by the G. I. Bill of Rights. I decided to major in philosophy.

We lived inexpensively in a Hyde Park townhouse rented from Theodora's father and shared with her sister and brother-in-law, who also had two small children. One Sunday Father Carrabine came visiting. When I told him about the frustrating trip to New York, he was most sympathetic. As director of Chicago Inter-Student Catholic Action (CISCA), he suggested that we might consider revising our idea, giving the publication a student angle, and publishing under the auspices of CISCA.

I had always taken a fairly dim view of the pietistic aims of CISCA; on the other hand, it had a great deal of influence in the Catholic high schools and colleges of the area and made the wartime dream of our own publication a distinct possibility. Anyway, we ended up enthusiastically accepting Father Carrabine's offer.

To be as up-to-the-minute as possible was one of our journalistic aims with *Today* (that is what we ended up calling our publication). It seemed to some of our readers, however, that we were shockingly contemporary and youthfully impious. We wrote about everything under the sun, reams of copy about subjects we had only a book knowledge of. Father Carrabine gave us the freedom we needed for our social crusades, our wars against sentimentality in religion, and our satiric treatments of advertising, book clubs, television, and other popular preoccupations.

The next three years were the busiest period of my whole life. It was a time of mourning. Both Theodora's mother and my father died during this period. It was also a time of never-ending activity. In addition to editing the now national *Today*, I attended Loyola full-time. I also lectured at various schools and on Saturdays to the nuns at the Sheil School of Social Studies. For a semester I taught a course in modern literature at St. Xavier's College under the watchful eye of a monitoring Sister of Mercy.

At home, the two little ones were growing in grace. In April of 1948, soon after I finally received my degree from Loyola, we had another son, Christopher. It was then more than a decade since I had taken the first class leading to a degree.

My Jesuit education was, of course, altogether too parochial in its interpretation of historical events, philosophy, and literature. The failings of the Catholic education offered in that day have been widely publicized and bear no repeating. However, despite its parochial limitations, I must say that the education offered at Loyola was superb. Its excellence was not due merely to the fabled urbanity of the Jesuits (I rarely had one of them as a teacher), but to the comprehensive plan of education in the Society of Jesus' famous *ratio studiorium*. We went through the classical periods of Greece and Rome, early Christianity, the European Middle Ages, the Reformation, the Enlightenment, and what followed. All this, to be sure, from a narrowly Roman Catholic point of view; but we did learn about these high points of Western civilization. Foreign cultures, like the Oriental and the African, were ignored. However, that was also true in almost every American college and university, religious or secular.

Soon after graduating from Loyola, I was paging through my father-in-law's set of the *Encyclopaedia Britannica*—an old habit—and ran across "Switzerland." The place sounded beautiful, peaceful, and marvelously unhurried. I knew that the University of Fribourg there specialized in Thomistic philosophy. By this time, I concluded, I was ready to tackle anything any school had to offer along that line.

I quickly decided that we would all go to Europe. *Today*—which was to last for the next twenty-five years—was well launched; at least it was on as solid a footing as it ever would be. There was nothing to keep us in Chicago.

The trip across the Atlantic on the *Queen Mary* was leisurely. The young director of the ship's gym insisted that Theodora try all his latest equipment. When she had to refuse, he demanded to know why. He was thoroughly embarrassed when she told him that she was pregnant and then added as a kind of afterthought that, other than her husband, he was the only one to know about the new baby.

When we landed at Le Havre, I was excited to step at last on European soil. Though I have returned to Europe numerous times since then, the feeling has returned each time.

There was a taxi strike in Paris and so, with bags and young children bearing down on us, we took the Métro to a small, most undesirable hotel. There was also a shortage of hotel rooms, the American Expressman explained. When the children were asleep in the dingy room he found for us, I went out on the street to savor the urbanity of Paris and try to arrange for better housing the next day.

I knew no French so, in order not to get lost, I carefully wrote down our present place, Hotel Meublé, which, I learned later, means roughly the same as "Furnished Rooms." However, I successfully arranged for housing at the not very appropriately named Hotel Moderne, a second-class hostel, but infinitely superior to the dreary room we had.

In Switzerland, in contrast to what we had left, everything was neat, orderly, and available. We were taken immediately to our apartment, a fifth-floor walkup. It was sparsely furnished but spotlessly clean, and there were sleeping accommodations for all except the new baby. But she was not yet with us and would not be for another seven months. When she did finally arrive, her bassinet was a drawer containing a pillow placed on top of a dresser.

The next day I went over to the university to get the new catalogue. Going over it, I discovered that the courses I wanted most were given in the theology faculty. I also learned from the Dominican dean that no student had ever been admitted to that faculty who was not a prospective Roman Catholic ordinand. With three children and the fourth coming, I hardly qualified. However, that exclusion was merely the ancient tradition. The only rule was that every new theology student had to have a letter of recommendation from his home bishop. I wrote immediately to Bishop Sheil in Chicago, who was familiar with my work on *Today*. He answered right away, with the prized commendation.

There was still the problem of Latin, the language of instruction. I had not studied Latin for years, but the Servites apparently had taught me well. With two weeks of brush-up work, I managed to pass the speaking-knowledge test the dean had arranged for me.

So it was that when classes opened, there was one married layman among the dozens of robed celibates from many nations who were in the great *aula*, ready to participate with them in classes in various areas of Thomistic studies and later to join in their vigorous Latin debates during the smaller seminars. I was even allowed to attend more classes than the fall course called for and mastered enough French, thanks largely to popular French films, to take courses in more secular subjects.

Terence and Ann went to one of the local kindergartens and soon surprised both of us by chattering away in childish, Swiss-accented French as if they were native to the land. Chris smiled happily in his crib. Our lives seemed peaceful and unusually uneventful. We thoroughly enjoyed the mountain beauty of our surroundings and were quieted down by the orderly progress of Swiss life. Of course, we were also awaiting the birth of the baby, who arrived on schedule in May—another daughter, Joan.

My most memorable professor in the theology faculty was a brusque Polish Dominican named Father Bochenski—an internationally established authority on both Marxism and symbolic logic. Some of Bochenski's best classes were informal sessions held in a public *bierstube*, where the price for asking him an abstruse question in philosophy or theology was to buy beer for the whole class. Bochenski appeared in his white habit, the students in their clerical gowns, and it was indeed very medieval. Quite a contrast to Chicago.

Bochenski's course, like all the others, allowed for little that was explicable except in the Thomistic framework. Father Bochenski himself, however, was never a serious offender in this regard, since he was quite aware of modern trends in philosophy. Some of the other faculty members, however, had rational Thomistic explanations for just about everything in Christian theology. For instance, one thesis claimed that there is no "accident" (as opposed to "substance") in God. God's knowledge of himself, therefore, must be a substance—in the divine case the substance is necessarily a person, the second member of the Holy Trinity. The inevitable love between these two must be still another personal substance, the Holy Spirit. The dogmatic teaching is that the Trinity is a revealed mystery of Christian faith, inaccessible to human reason, so the argument was not taken very seriously.

Such rigid rationalism, however, intrigued me. I was not bad at playing the Thomistic game. But for the first time in my life, studiously and admiringly reading the *Summa Theologica*, I was actually tempted to nontheistic disbelief. It was the same way years later: Newman's *Apologia pro Vita Sua* only led me away from Rome and toward Canterbury.

The experience of living in a small Swiss town—almost all Roman Catholic, with cassocked and habited seminarians everywhere—was a sharp contrast to the pace of irreligious Chicago. Roman Catholicism was taken for granted in Fribourg, which proudly called itself a second Rome because of the many old religious houses and seminaries in the area. For instance, one did not need to explain Roman Catholic references that might have required painful exegesis elsewhere. There was no bafflement such as was expressed by Saul Alinsky, who once told me that he could make nothing but obscene sense out of a promise of five hundred "ejaculations" offered him in writing by a group of nuns he had supported in a political dispute.

One day a saintly Dominican professor looked out over the dozens of students gathered in the lecture hall. He envisioned aloud the future when the students then together there would be scattered throughout the world as pastors, foreign missionaries, novice masters, university professors, perhaps even as bishops and cardinals in the Roman Curia. Clearly for my sake, the lone layman, he suggested that the laity, too, had an important role to play in the world and that they might be found doing almost anything. I, too, could serve the cause of the Church if I wished to, despite my vocational handicap, by assisting my clerical betters and upholding the true position when no priest was around to state Catholic teaching.

Later, during the great exodus from the priesthood and the religious life of the 1960s, I wondered how many of the earnest, robed young men who were then in the theology classroom in Fribourg were now the busy fathers of families, and how many were pastors and foreign missionaries.

I learned a great deal, of course, not only in classes at the university but through frequent trips around Europe. Both Theodora and I had lived in many places, so we were exposed to various communities throughout the United States. But we knew nothing about Europe. I don't think affection for our native land decreased with these experiences; it probably grew. But there was something about Europe that I in particular found most congenial. I never felt like a stranger anywhere, even though I might be totally ignorant of the language and pitifully gauche in the social manners expected of me.

Still I was anything but loathe to return to the United States, where I had a job waiting for me. An army friend had just been appointed by President Truman to head a new Federal Commission in Washington, and had asked me to be his executive assistant. After the summer school, we left for France and boarded the *Ile de France* for the trip back home. Of course travel was even more cumbersome since we had added tiny Joan to an already large family group. And we were quite broke as well, but for us that was not unusual. I learned that there was a check waiting for me at *Commonweal* for an article reprint, so I went over to the New York office to pick it up.

While there, Ed Skillin, the editor-in-chief, offered me a job—much to my surprise. I would replace Philip Burnham, the executive editor, who was leaving the magazine. The job would pay sixty dollars a week. I was eager to accept the editorial position. Such work had always intrigued me, and meant settling in the New York area instead of around Washington, and making a great deal less money. But, I reasoned, it also offered personal satisfaction such as I could never achieve in the Washington bureaucracy.

We returned to Chicago with the understanding that a month later I would be back in New York as an editor of *Commonweal*. Years later, when I became an Anglican, Father Andrew Greeley wrote that my going East was the beginning of the end for a man unusually well trained to be a lay leader in the Roman Catholic Church.

CHAPTER V

Commonweal

THE first issue I ever worked on at *Commonweal* was an out-sized anniversary issue marking the magazine's silver jubilee. There were also two recently hired graduates of Notre Dame on the staff: Edward Meagher and William Pfaff. I did not get Philip Burnham's job, as I thought I would, nor his title of executive editor. My title, it seemed, had to be lower than that of Mr. Meagher, who was designated in the masthead as managing editor. I was called feature editor, a meaningless title.

Meagher was something of a perfectionist. He was from Seattle, and remained an unreformed westerner in New York, the citadel of eastern urban culture. Meagher was never really happy at *Commonweal*, and his discontent pervaded the office. There were so many disagreements, so much dissension, pouting, and group tension that the situation soon became unbearable. In less than a year, I was ready to quit and seek a new job in order to support my growing family. When I announced this, Meagher (who had always remained personally friendly) told me that no matter what I did he was going to move on—probably back to Seattle. He urged me to reconsider the decision, since Pfaff would soon be drafted for the Korean War, and without me *Commonweal* would lack an experienced editor. I agreed to stay on.

Meagher left, I stayed, and Pfaff went into the army—all as had been anticipated. For a few months Ed Skillin and I put out the magazine alone. Then James O'Gara, my former confrère from the *Catholic Worker* and *Today*, joined us in New York as managing editor.

After Meagher left, I was given the title I had originally been led to expect—executive editor.

A few months later, in 1952, we were joined by William Clancy, a Notre Dame professor who had already written a *Commonweal* article on Catholic censorship and "The Miracle" case. Clancy was then winding up his twenties. He was well versed in ecclesiastical history and went along with our own attitude toward popular American Catholicism. Clancy lived in Greenwich Village and counted among his acquaintances Norman Mailer, Michael Harrington, Dylan Thomas, Jules Pfeiffer, and Montgomery Clift. He lived a sophisticated urban life and was very much a part of the Village scene in the fifties. Several years later he became an Oratorian priest.

I became a columnist for *Commonweal* in a strange way. There came a day, of course, when sixty dollars a week was an impossible salary for a man who had six other persons to support—another child, Paul, was born during this period and Mark, our sixth and last, was on the way. My intention at first was simply to get a better-paying job. But Ed Skillin had another idea. There would be no raise in salary, for that would set a bad precedent, he said. However, if I wrote a signed column I could be paid fifteen dollars extra every week. It would require two weekly checks. I went along with this fiction for almost three years. The column continued, off and on, for more than a decade after I left the staff of *Commonweal*.

During my years at *Commonweal*, I was frequently summoned to be the Roman Catholic in the usual Protestant-Catholic-Jewish teams that were assembled to mark Religious Emphasis Week in various secular colleges around the United States. I played a similar role on television. A priest might have been more desirable, but Roman Catholic priests at that time were forbidden to participate with clergymen of other faiths in public appearances, no matter how secular the theme. I also lectured at Yale, Cornell, Notre Dame, Fordham, Columbia, Chicago, and various other universities.

Occasionally, my columns were picked up by the daily press, and I was asked to expand others for such periodicals as *Look*, the *New York Herald Tribune*, the Sunday *Times*, and other publications. I wrote book reviews regularly for the local New York papers and somehow found time to contribute to the Jesuits' *America* and other Roman Catholic publications. *Collier's* sent me to Rome to figure out who would succeed Pius XII. (I dismissed Cardinal Roncalli as much too old to deserve serious attention!)

With Harold Fey of the *Christian Century* and Morris Lazaron, a retired rabbi, I traveled for weeks in six countries throughout the Middle East, where we interviewed kings and prime ministers, and many poverty-stricken refugees. We returned home with our reports on what we had witnessed during stops in Egypt, Lebanon, Syria, Turkey, Jordan, and Israel. In Washington we reported directly to a distracted John Foster Dulles, then Secretary of State.

Life at *Commonweal* was not usually so eventful; it was fairly routine, in fact. In addition to my full share in choosing articles, editing them, assigning books for review, and writing the weekly column, I worked on my own for Bishop Sheil of Chicago.

Sheil had sent for me one day, and I flew west to meet him for lunch. He explained that he needed someone to "polish" the many speeches he was being called upon to make. To put it bluntly, he proposed, without saying it in so many words, that I should be his ghost writer. The pay would be the truly princely sum of one thousand dollars a month. I accepted with alacrity.

The most important speech I ever wrote for Sheil was a highly publicized one denouncing Joe McCarthy. It was Sheil's own idea. When I asked him how far he wanted to go in his denunciation of "that fellow," he said "All the way! Full steam ahead!" I cheerfully went "all the way" that very night, working alone at the kitchen table.

I sent the speech off to Chicago and waited. Sheil, in his characteristic forgetfulness, had long since ceased to pay me; but this was a labor of love. I was very disturbed about the effect McCarthy was having on the nation and thought it past time that a highly placed cleric should counteract the effect of the Catholic chorus of approval of Joseph McCarthy.

The speech I wrote was given at a United Automobile Workers meeting. It caused a national sensation. Reports on it led off the television news and it was reprinted in its entirety. Sheil was featured on the air several times and received thousands of congratulatory letters and telegrams.

I did not hear from him again for weeks. By that time, he had accumulated the positive communications, which he showed me proudly. During the long silence, I had a sociable drink one afternoon with Saul Alinsky, who was visiting Manhattan. He told me, in strictest confidence of course, that *he* had written the McCarthy speech for Bishop Sheil. Keeping the secret was most difficult for me under such circumstances.

The special arrangements with Sheil went on for only a short time after the McCarthy speech. It died after I rejected one of his requests for a speech that I did not have time to write. I was a candidate for Congress and needed public speeches for myself.

This was the decade when Paul Blanshard's warnings against the supposed subversive intent of the Roman Catholic Church hit the best-seller lists. It was also a period when both the United States and the Roman Catholic Church were hounded by doubts about their own security and preoccupied by a supposed internal infiltration by members of the Communist Party.

The inevitable result was a certain amount of unspoken collaboration. It was well known, for instance, that graduates of Catholic colleges were preferred as FBI men over the products of Yale or Harvard. The CIA was a generous supporter of a number of Catholic ventures overseas. The original article by Vincent Hartnett which launched the blacklisting of people in the radio, television, and entertainment fields appeared in *The Sign*, a monthly published by the Passionist Fathers.

From both civic and religious viewpoints, it was a crucial period to be an editor of *Commonweal*. We did not go along with the dominant mood in either church or state; consequently, we were held in widespread disrepute by both.

Our politics, no more than our theology, were not really very radical. On both scores, *Commonweal* turned to the left in the next stormy decade but without stirring up as much enmity as our mild liberalism did in the fifties.

I would not be prepared to say that, in our time, *Commonweal* was really a model of far-seeing progressive thought. There were clear vestiges of the ongoing anti-communist myths in its pages during that period, and there was a theological timidity that *Commonweal* later repudiated. We were not as outspoken on some subjects as we later became. This was mainly due to the conservative spirit of the times, not to any directives from above. The ecclesiastical authorities left us alone, and there was a great deal of freedom among ourselves.

At that time, thanks mainly to Edward Skillin's gentle permissiveness, the custom was that any individual editor, for any reason, had the right to veto anything that might be submitted. We did not always agree on everything that was finally published. Nevertheless, in the five years I was with the magazine, this editorial veto power was never invoked.

As far as our own Catholicity went, we were incurable essentialists. The actual behavior of Church leaders and prominent prelates might be somewhat embarrassing to such hardy civic libertarians, but in dismissing it as irrelevant, we could always fall back on a platonic notion of the Church.

The Roman Curia might be reactionary, it might be the era of *Humani Generis*, and some of the strongest voices in the Church might be forcibly silenced—such matters had nothing to do with the spirit of liberty and progress we believed lurked, unexpressed, in some recondite theological teachings. When a group of Catholics picketed the Metropolitan Opera because a priest-character was shown in a bad light, we agreed that the protest was silly. But we anathematized it as a "perversion" of true Catholicism because the Church had always put heavy emphasis on art in its teachings.

As far as Catholic disciplinary practices went, it never crossed our minds to challenge most of them publicly. There was a mild advocacy of vernacular in the liturgy in our pages, but that is about as far as we were ready to go. No challenging, for instance, of clerical celibacy, or of excluding women from Holy Orders.

We took the absolute prohibitions against divorce and contraception as clear demands of the gospel or of natural law. There was no talk about the individual's right to act according to his own conscience and practice birth control, though we knew many Catholics who secretly did just that. A priest once told me in the confessional that if sleeping with a wife was too tempting for a young man who already had a large family and felt he could not afford more, abstinence was the only solution. He recommended that the couple sleep apart, in separate beds, apparently regardless of the effect such an arrangement might have on the marriage itself. One of our associates constantly, though in a jocular "Catholic" spirit, referred to a divorced friend's second wife as his "whore."

This may sound unbearably censorious and unforgiving. But actually, people who talked this way were sometimes more compassionate and understanding than many outside the Church who took a very tolerant position, in theory. Most Catholics, however, were simply not ready to judge moral acts other than by this traditional code.

We were quite aware that all Catholics were not so rigid in their interpretation of duty as we were—that much was evident. But they would be saved, happily, by their ignorance. Those who were as well trained in the principles of natural law as we were, for instance, were bound to strict adherence to it; others simply did not recognize the extent of their duty.

These early years of the fifties passed quickly. At home, there was

enough work with the children to keep Theodora and me fully occupied. We were proud of our big, handsome family. One Saturday
morning I did the usual bathing and dressing chores assumed by
almost every father of a young family. Then I hurried off to a large
Communion breakfast at a parish in Queens. One of the Jesuit editors
of *America* and I were to be the speakers. Before we were introduced,
the pastor of the parish lauded his young curate to the skies and
mentioned in passing, unfortunately, no one could expect to learn
anything from the invited speakers—"highbrows" who knew nothing about the realities of life and had no contact with children. I was
very put off and could barely wait to get out of the place. The Jesuit
took the implied insult philosophically and laughed it off. However, I
never again spoke at a parish gathering.

Through Bill Clancy, I got to know Wayne Cowan of *Christianity and
Crisis*, Arthur Moore of *Methodist Outlook*, Arthur Cohen of Meridian
Books; all young men who gathered at the White Horse Tavern in
Greenwich Village. I, too, took to staying in town one night a week. I
would have dinner with Clancy, talking furiously about the issues of
the day, and usually ending up at the White Horse, where we engaged in primitive ecumenical dialogue with these friends.

My getting into local politics was probably the beginning of the end
of this pleasant phase of my life. In any case, before the election of
1954, when I was a Democratic candidate of Congress, I had left
Commonweal for good.

My entry into politics was marvelously simple. One day I received a
phone call from a leader of the Democratic Party in our heavily Re-
publican district of Nassau County, offering me the next-to-useless
Congressional spot on the national ticket. At most, my candidacy
would provide me with another platform to carry on a personal pro-
civil liberties stand.

I actually left the staff of *Commonweal* in September, 1954, when I
undertook, as an independent agent, to direct a study on blacklisting
in the entertainment fields for the Fund for the Republic. I did not, of
course, realize at that time how very long that relationship would go
on. During most of my long employment, I continued the column for
Commonweal and became more and more associated in people's minds
not with the Fund but with *Commonweal*. Even today, friends are
surprised to learn that I was an editor of the magazine for only a short
time and was with the Fund for the Republic for more than two
decades.

All during my stay at *Commonweal*, we were hounded by our need for money. The circulation was very small and the little good will we enjoyed in the Roman Catholic community was unreliable. During the years since then I have often met people who tell me about what sturdy support they personally gave the weekly in the lonely fifties. I must have run across nearly twenty thousand subscribers and several dozen financial supporters. But to my knowledge supporters were rare.

Leaving *Commonweal* meant going from a penny-pinching, starving weekly to one of the fabulously rich spin-offs of the Ford Foundation.

REFLECTION TWO

As an editor of Commonweal, *I had a distinct position in the Roman Catholic community. In those days, however, there was such a creature as a "Commonweal Catholic," and they were considered to be outside the pale. I certainly did not feel like a special kind of Catholic nor did my confrères, but our ventures into the normal society of Catholicism were nevertheless few and far between. There was likely to be an embarrassing incident or a pointedly snide remark which we were eager to avoid.*

We really tried from time to time to figure out what was intended by calling people "Commonweal Catholics." The designation had nothing to do with religious observance. Rather, the idea was spread abroad that any group which consistently criticized Senator Joe McCarthy, gave unfavorable reviews to Cardinal Spellman's novel, and took a dim view of the Legion of Decency's moralistic simplicity, might be Catholic in name and orthodox in faith, but certainly was not Catholic "enough." Popular Catholicism in those days was not seriously bigoted, but it did represent a tight, cohesive group and demanded the kind of loyalty we were not prepared to offer.

The Church seemed to have a clear position on almost everything under the sun. These positions were certainly not held as formally authoritative or beyond debate; but they were treated as if they were revealed by the Holy Spirit directly. To question one, even though it was permissibly debatable, was simply not done.

One problem was that to many Catholics it all seemed to go together—trust in the sacred powers of Lourdes water, belief in the Trinity of the Godhead, observance of the seeemingly infinite number of marital regulations in Canon Law, and the Commandment proscribing adultery.

More than that, a specific list of favored persons and customs received sanctification that one might legitimately argue about with the clergy but which usually went blissfully unchallenged. For instance, I remember being lambasted once by the Brooklyn Tablet *because I had referred in print to a Benedictine writer as simply Mariella Gable, without putting "Sister" before her name. Once an Episcopal priest called on us at* Commonweal *and introduced himself as "Father," and our Irish receptionist pointedly announced the visitor as "Doctor."*

There was a certain discomfort among the editors for being free of this largely self-imposed ghettoization, though we felt sure that Catholic isolation was on the way out. We were prepared to recognize the effects of the recent war, when millions of laymen and thousands of priests had lived for years side by side as military equals with non-Catholic Americans who did not under-stand Roman Catholic habits, peculiarities of speech, or thought patterns. Also, the vast postwar exodus to the suburbs meant that old religious citadels in the big cities were breaking down. Unless there is an unexpected reversal, the Roman Catholic community in the United States will never again display the kind of cohesiveness that gave it its last hurrahs: first to Al Smith, then to Joe McCarthy, and later to John F. Kennedy.

What can be said for the Catholic ghetto mentality while it lasted? For one thing, it helped a vast group of Americans in their adjustments to life in a nation that was not always congenial to them or to their ancient culture. It controlled envy by setting up Catholic celebrities, literature, awards, honors, and even a Who's Who. *It became painfully aware that its own scholarly accomplishments were severely limited, but it made up for that by claiming that, at least in theology, it alone had the full truth, and that in moral matters all its basic answers were perennially authentic.*

The breakup of the ghetto pattern was a slow process. It was not openly challenged until Pope John XXIII came along. Its final demise is still not completed, but there are things being said from pulpits today that would have been unthinkable before the Second Vatican Council. Everyone, from the liberated editors of the National Catholic Reporter *to the die-hard old liturgists of Father De Pauw's conservative movement, has loosened up. In addition, not long ago the National Opinion Research group at the Univer-sity of Chicago revealed that American Catholics and Jews now outranked white Protestants in both education and income.*

I do not think we will ever again read of priests rushing into burning churches to "rescue" the Blessed Sacrament, or hear of uncloistered sisters being forbidden to attend family weddings. But some of the old attitudes still hold fast. One Roman Curia officer recently said that much depends on the next pope. Paul VI, compared to Pius XII, has been a remarkably liberal pontiff. He has authorized changes in the Church that are felt in every parish. But if Pope Paul is judged by all that was expected of John XXIII's successor, he will be seen as wanting, for he is himself caught up in the traditionalist training he received as a youth and is not quite attuned to the new theology.

His greatest folly was Humanae Vitae. *This encyclical actually need not have been written. In two strongholds of Roman Catholicism—Europe and America—Catholics were already practicing birth control and, with priestly approval, millions continued in good conscience to do so after the document was released. The big difference the encyclical actually made was that the pope lost a great deal of credibility after it was released. It was generally acknowl-edged, even by its supporters, that the document was not infallible. But in that case it served little purpose other than to put forth an already well known opinion in a world that had moved on from the days when procreation, and procreation alone, justified marital sex. Only with difficulty could* Humanae Vitae *be squared with the Vatican Council's endorsement of "responsible parenthood." It had to be based on the idea that indefinitely prolonged absti- nence was to be considered the norm for Roman Catholic couples.*

There is no doubt that there have been times in history when the extraordi- nary claims of the Bishop of Rome served Christendom well. Along with the memory of the "bad" popes, one should, in fairness, keep in mind those pontiffs, like John XXIII, who have honored the office–and there were quite a few of them.

My own loss of faith in the papacy as a divinely established institution in the Church had little to do with Pope Paul's 1968 encyclical. About this time, though, one heard more and more priests declaring that they paid little or no attention to the sovereign pontiff, unless he was speaking "infallibly"—and that will probably never happen again.

I certainly was not impressed with the few results of infallible pronounce- ments, and I was distressed that Paul thought it wise to state even a non- infallible opinion on a vital moral question affecting the welfare of an already overcrowded planet. It was clear to me that by the time of Humanae Vitae *I no longer accepted the papal claim to infallibility.*

The ideal of celibacy for all the clergy, I came to realize, was based on a cultic image of the priesthood which was on its way out. The priest was not considered an officer of the Christian community so much as a "holy man" who must remain "unsullied" by sex if he is allowed to represent the Chris- tian sacrifice. That, of course, was no longer my concept of either the priest- hood or sex, but clearly it still dominated thinking in clerical Rome.

After 1968 and that fatal encyclical, I began to look more to the Episcopal Church. Two Anglican bishops, E. Edward Crowther and James Pike, were fellow workers with me at that time. Neither of them, however, had even mildly suggested that I should transfer my Christian allegiance to their communion. Still, more and more often I found myself attending Episcopal services as well as my own Roman Catholic ones. I felt better at the Anglican liturgy because I was not called upon to profess credence in any dogma I no longer believed, and I was not expected to hold as true anything ambiguously "proved" by the Scriptures.

The Roman and Anglican Eucharists, now that Rome at long last had instituted the vernacular in the liturgy, were very similar, though Anglicans avoided all references to purgatory, to non-Scripturally recorded events of Mary's life, and the primal position of the Bishop of Rome.

I was pleased at this, not so much because I denied them—Mary might have been conceived without original sin and her body might have been assumed into heaven—but merely because I had no way of knowing for sure.

CHAPTER VI

Blacklist Report

DURING the last year at *Commonweal*, I had lunch regularly with Leo Rosten of *Look* magazine. One day I confessed to Rosten that I was interested in a more secular job. I was growing tired of the humiliations of being a maverick lay Catholic editor, even though we were definitely not an ecclesiastical publication, as the local chancery had recently made clear to the general press.

A few days later, Rosten suggested that I go over to see Robert M. Hutchins of the Fund for the Republic, at the Lincoln Building. Hutchins, he said, had something in mind that I might be qualified for.

Of course, like every other Chicagoan of my generation, I had heard of Bob Hutchins, but I had never met him. Theodora had attended the University of Chicago during the period when Hutchins had been the much-publicized president there. What I did not know was that the Fund for the Republic was a spin-off of the Ford Foundation and that Hutchins was the Fund's recently elected president. Neither did I have it clear that the Fund and the Ford Foundation were now independent organizations.

I went to the Fund's modern offices as arranged, and met the distinguished Hutchins and his cocky number two man, W. H. (Ping) Ferry. A few days earlier the Fund's board had authorized a study of blacklisting in the entertainment industries and had assigned one hundred thousand dollars for that purpose. Hutchins offered me the job of directing the investigation. I could pick my own staff, write the final report, and was expected to tell nothing but the unvarnished truth. The job would not be of long duration, but then, Hutchins indicated, neither would the Fund.

At the time the Fund was lavishly spending the fifteen million dollars it had been given by the Ford Foundation, making large grants to the Southern Regional Council, the League of Women Voters, the Catholic Interracial Council of Chicago, and dozens of other groups organized to combat racial segregation or attacks on American civil liberties. The organization's true charter, Hutchins often stated, was the Declaration of Independence and the Constitution of the United States. He called it an "anti-absurdity" endowment.

I told Hutchins and Ferry that there was just one small problem—I was already a Congressional candidate. When I added that I was running as a Democrat in Nassau County, he half-heartedly wished me luck and said that I could begin with the Fund after the dismal returns came in.

I left the office, then, with a new job. At first I only took a leave of absence from *Commonweal*, nominally to concentrate on the Congressional campaign. In the meantime, I hired for the Fund project a young man I knew from the *Catholic Worker* and the White Horse Tavern. He was Michael Harrington, who later gained national fame as the author of *The Other America*. Harrington, himself a socialist, knew the ins and outs of the Communist Party better than any non-communist of my acquaintance. He could readily distinguish between members of the Party and the principles upon which the Party itself was founded. He was then just twenty-six, a product of Holy Cross, Yale, and the University of Chicago. I could not have made a more compassionate or less gullible first choice than this young Marxist.

We started off by going to Hollywood to assemble a West Coast staff and also to find out what we could learn in the movie studios. Our entrée into the industry was limited. We took the night plane (Harrington in a new suit purchased for him on a credit card by my colleague Bill Clancy). Hours later, we were having an elegant lunch at the old Universal studios.

The only person I knew in the industry was a man named Gordon, since deceased, who had once put through a telephone call to *Commonweal* and got me on the line. His job was to go over scripts and even finished pictures to make sure they were acceptable by the formidable Catholic Legion of Decency. For instance, in those days movie sin had to be clearly punished in this life, so he saw to it that scripts provided for sudden deaths, fatal accidents, and suicides. To manage all this well, Gordon had to be something of an authority on Catholic Canon Law and the subtleties of Roman moral theology.

When we arrived in Los Angeles, I telephoned him, and he invited us to have lunch with him in the studio commissary the very next day. There, in an unaccustomed glamorous setting, with famous faces scattered around the room, we confessed to him why we were in Hollywood.

Gordon was most sympathetic and advised us to make contact with a man named Mendel Silberberg, a Harvard-trained lawyer who was informally authorized to speak for the whole industry. He also assured us that there was indeed a blacklist in Hollywood. The air in town was poisoned by it, he said. But he warned us that those in power would deny there was such a list. Behind closed doors, however, they might admit discriminating against communists, communist sympathizers, and even people who might once have innocently signed an injudicious petition or contributed to Russian relief during the war.

Almost everyone in the industry was against the practice, he said, but few movie people were brave enough to take on its powerful proponents. Most bore the stigma of unemployment without public complaint, hoping that in time they could be "cleared" by some articulate anti-communist, right-wing columnist, or union activist and again be eligible for work.

To gain absolution they had of course to do their share of penance. This might include appearing before a meeting of the House Un-American Activities Committee or the Internal Security subcommittee of the Senate, or by naming others. Or it might include voting "correctly" at a union meeting, or signing an anti-communist article written for a big-name star by one of Hollywood's professional anti-communists. Of course such behavior inevitably led to the poisoning of human relations in the motion picture industry.

We could have written the report that day. Gordon had given us all the essential data at our first luncheon. But of course we had to verify what he said and document the charges.

Before I left California we had interviews with a number of industry leaders, including the paternalistic Silberberg himself, a soft-voiced patrician Ivy Leaguer who opened doors for us that might otherwise have remained firmly closed. One way or another, all of them—even Silberberg—verified Gordon's account. The head of one important studio frankly told us, for instance, that when a name came up he simply consulted Congress's anti-communist hearings and decided if the person was employable according to whether his name appeared on the index. We learned later that he sometimes made notable exceptions.

One rising young star had been reared in a solid Marxist background. As she grew up, the *Daily Worker* was around the house and her membership in the party's children's groups was taken for granted by the family. Still, when her name appeared in one of the fatal indices, she told the studio head that she really knew nothing about communism. In a word, she played the "dumb blonde" she had enacted so credibly on film. To the producer she recited her lines as if the script had been prepared for her. The head, of course, knew better, but millions of dollars of studio money were at stake. He feigned complete belief in her story, and the star went on to make several profitable pictures.

It was well known in the motion picture industry at the time that some previously high-paid writers were officially blacklisted but nonetheless were actually writing scripts under pseudonyms—for greatly reduced fees, of course. One of these men later confessed to me that he anonymously wrote a movie about a group of nuns which was extravagantly praised by the right-wing Catholic press.

One of those hit by the blacklist was Jane Wyatt, a person I had reason to know was anything but a communist. She came from an established family and was among the few American aristocrats with a Roman Catholic background. When her agent suspected that she was being blacklisted because she had originally supported the Hollywood Ten, he took her to a priest, who later cheerfully vouched for her loyalty with officials of the American Legion. Soon after that, offers came in again.

Back home in New York, after the short stay in California, I threw my efforts into serious campaigning. I did not really have a chance to defeat the veteran incumbent, Frank J. Becker, but I went all out during the campaign. By my lights, Becker was a crypto-McCarthyite. I thought that was reason enough for him to be retired from the House.

Because I was clearly the anti-McCarthy candidate in the area, I gained the helpful support of most of the writers and television personalities who lived on Long Island. For the next few weeks, I talked everywhere in the district—in fire stations, schools, churches, parking lots, Levittown living rooms—just about anywhere listeners could be assembled. My opponent was stirred from his usual campaign lethargy. He attacked me as wholly inexperienced, which was quite true, and accused me of injecting religion into the campaign, which was absolutely false. On the contrary, I had resisted all efforts to exploit my Catholic associations. For instance, I refused to be photographed by *Newsday* attending Mass on Sunday with my family.

The campaign has grown dim in my memory, but I recall getting lost frequently in the wilds of Long Island suburbs, frantically driving up and down tree-lined streets in the knowledge that a group of supporters in one of the look-alike living rooms was waiting for its candidate to appear. The political experience—my first—was instructive and edifying. My chances were so slight that I could promise nothing to supporters. Yet the energy, money, and enthusiastic work with which supporters who had nothing to gain backed up the campaign were tremendous.

It was a relief to return to anonymity, however. I was delighted when they removed the billboards with my name and picture on them. Actually, I was quite pleased that I would not have to take on the burdens of political office, though I would have been prepared to do so.

Now there was nothing to stop me from engaging full time in the blacklisting study. Mike Harrington had not left the West Coast before signing up Paul Jacobs, an anti-Stalinist radical writer; and Elizabeth Poe Kerby and Dorothy B. Jones, experienced researchers. At home, we quickly added to the New York staff James Greene, over-all secretary; Ed Engberg, a former *Fortune* reporter; Margaret Bushong, a long-time *Time* researcher; Saul Blackman, a labor organizer; Gwendolyn Boulkind, a general reporter; and Harriet Davis, a veteran radio factotum. Marie Jahoda, sociologist of New York University, directed an independent study.

We thought it best to establish an office quite separate from the sponsoring Fund itself and rented rooms at the Shelton Hotel. To these rooms there came a steady procession of blacklisted radio and television personnel, to be interviewed at length. A few of them were, in time, reinstated. Now and then I still see them on television. At least two of them have become major stars in maturity.

Most of the people ready to talk about their own histories were the writers, technicians, and character actors whose names were never known to the public. A few were, or had once been, members of the Communist Party; more, however, were fuzzy liberals who had been casual about the causes they sponsored. A few were the victims of a simple mistake in names.

In Hollywood the story was the same. There the blacklisting apparatus was even more rigidly structured. Almost everyone employed at the major studios had written a letter stating that he was not now and had never been a member of the Communist Party. If he had been, he had some explaining to do. These explanations were made to a group of self-appointed guardians of the nation's security. Hundreds of people were involved.

We worked on both coasts, amassing a vast amount of material. We surveyed industry leaders and advertisers by mail. Most of them flatly denied that there was a blacklist, and then went on to say in one way or another that their obedience to its demands was justified, patriotically and commercially.

The blacklisters themselves were also contacted. We wanted to present their side of the story fairly. I remember especially the most "professional" of these—Vincent Hartnett. For a fee, Hartnett released the names of show people with dubious associations and then, for a second fee, "cleared" those he had named. He admitted on the stand in the John Henry Faulk case that over the years he had amassed one hundred thousand dollars by such a procedure.

Hartnett struck me as something of a fanatic. He undertook this for money, true, but his main motivation seemed to be ideological commitment. Others, like the columnists George Sokolsky and Victor Riesel, were more worldly-wise. They said they saw something downright virtuous in creating a "climate of employability" for persons who asked for their blessing. Since they were so well known as anti-communists, their statement that so-and-so had become a patriotic citizen meant that people like the powerful supermarket owner of Syracuse, Laurance Johnson, would no longer be on the attack. These men felt a bit smug about their "clearance" operations and probably really believed that only muddleheaded liberalism could explain our objections to it. They regretted that there was sometimes a confusion of names, but were satisfied that such errors were kept to a minimum. Mistakes were tolerable if they were the price of keeping real communists off the air and screen.

During the summer months, I put the hundreds of interviews together and compiled a long report on what they had found. I presumed the report would finally be published. It was written immediately for the board of directors of the Fund for the Republic, a group of prominent worthies representing business, politics, religion, and education. They were the victims of the continuous bad press that was created by the indifference of Messrs. Hutchins and Ferry to what they airily referred to as anti-communist hysteria.

Later, when CBS itself produced "Fear on Trial"—John Henry Faulk's own account of his case—it seemed that Hutchins and Ferry were correct. However, the Fund's entire board certainly did not agree with them. Even some of the most liberal of civil libertarians among them were thrown off base by the unfavorable publicity that fell in on the Fund.

I was first told by board members that the report I had prepared was too lengthy for popular reading, though my tendency had been to underwrite rather than to overwrite. I went to work again, cutting down the report to an indisputably manageable size. Then it was proposed that the revised report be kept secret, and distribution limited to the entertainment executives on both coasts. After all, they were the only ones who could do anything about blacklisting.

I was opposed to such clandestine reporting. I knew I would be under pressure to publish what the researchers found: I knew we could not get away with selective circulation, and I told the board as much. They seemed to be impressed by my opinion and temporarily affected by Hutchins' nonconformity. After much argument they appropriated enough money to subsidize the publication of ten thousand copies of the two volumes.

The day finally came when the blacklist study was ready for release. It was front-paged across the country and led off the network news reports the night before. The first reviews were definitely favorable. Then came a flood of peevish notices and editorials. The New York Hearst paper, for instance, ran a highly critical editorial comment. The man who wrote it said privately that he had never even seen the books; that orders had come to him from above. Other journalists took their lead from him. Soon the notices were almost universally "mixed," gleefully pointing out minor inaccuracies or simply denouncing the Fund and Robert Maynard Hutchins. I was very unhappy about this reception and distressed that so many stories on the report suggested that Hutchins was the real culprit, though throughout he had been careful not to interfere.

A few days after the books came out, I was subpoenaed by an embarrassed process-server. The House Committee on Un-American Activities wanted to see me. I went to Washington, D.C. for what I thought would be a private session, but turned out to be public. I was met in a most friendly fashion by Congressman Eugene J. McCarthy, an old friend, who led me into the proper room, his hand on my shoulder, to express at least one legislator's contempt for the inquisitional proceedings.

Mr. Walter, the chairman of the commitee, was in and out of the room throughout the prolonged hearing. It was soon clear that the congressmen—sitting like a jury listening to the staffman, Mr. Arens, grill me—had not read either of the two books. Mr. Arens' questions were so outrageous that some of the representatives were uneasy. Arens demanded the names of my interviewees, of course, though I had solemnly promised I would not reveal them. I had chosen not to have counsel and I answered all but questions about the interviewees.

After hours of questioning, a committeeman asked politely if I wished to make a statement or ask a question. "Why," I asked, "am I here?" Arens had not impugned my own affiliations, and my presence must have been caused by some factor that bore on the legislation that the committee would have to recommend about subversion.

Mr. Walter ventured an official reply: "You are here," he said, "because the committee wanted to know if it would have reached the conclusions you reached had it undertaken a study of blacklisting."

I was finally dismissed; but the hearings themselves were continued in Philadephia. Witnesses at this meeting were a movie actress who, as the committee was sure, would take the Fifth Amendment, and a group that included most of those named in the books as "clearance men." They all roundly condemned me, and my work was variously described as "useless," "inaccurate," and a "comfort to the communists."

Finally, I thought, the long ordeal was over. I had grown sick of the word "blacklisting" and had refused to talk about it in public, though tempting lecture fees were offered by interested groups. I settled down to the routine of the office in the penthouse of Manhattan's Lincoln Building.

In January, 1956, I had become a member of the Fund's regular staff. I was given vaguely defined duties. The offices were crowded and we had to share rooms at first and use pool stenographers. I was new to the work but I quickly learned how to pass on applications for grants, my main task.

The Fund itself was getting a great deal of unfavorable publicity, thanks to Fulton Lewis, Jr., a powerful right-wing broadcaster, some of whose supporters were public spokesmen who occupied prominent positions and who also enjoyed the patronage of some key Congressional staff men. Hutchins set a fine example of indifference to the popular furor. He remained lofty and cool in his public manner but highly compassionate in personal dealings with the Fund staff, and always proper and gentlemanly whether in private or in public. We all admired him tremendously.

His chief associate, Ping Ferry, was deliberately brusque and tactless in his public statements, but extremely kind, even sentimental, in personal dealings. He caused great distress for the Fund secretary, Adam Yarmolinski, an orderly, liberal but cautious young man who was meticulous to a flaw and had taken his training at the Yale Law School very seriously. Another important associate of the Fund was David Freeman, a very conventional foundation officer who probably found Hutchins's and Ferry's defiant behavior something of a headache but was unfailingly courteous to them and to everyone else. It was a lively office—the center of continuous controversy in the media.

The Fund's daily work was boring and unsatisfying, however, and I was clearly in need of something more challenging than commenting on dozens of bureaucratically written appeals for grants. I found assembling the Fund's impressive "Three-Year Report" a wearying task. When I finally announced to Hutchins my intention to move on, he was surprisingly sympathetic. He said I was justifiably bored and asked me to stay around for a while; perhaps changes would soon be made. He was bored, too, he said.

What he had in mind was the establishment of a program called "Basic Issues," a long-time interdisciplinary dream going back to the University of Chicago and the fact that professors from different departments there had nothing but the weather to talk about at the faculty club.

Yarmolinsky and Freeman were still committed to the idea of the Fund as a grant-giving organization. It was Hutchins' idea to spend the remaining money on discovering the basic causes of disturbances like blacklisting, since only a few persons seemed exercised by the voluminous reports on the violations of civil liberties that the Fund had unearthed. In almost every case, the press was ready to argue about whether it was January 30 or 31, but little or no attention was paid to the underlying cause of these outrages—the basic issue.

I found Hutchins' idea exciting. But to turn our efforts in this direction we needed the board's permission. A great deal of staff dissension resulted when it was learned that the president intended to try to reverse our activities.

Yarmolinsky and Freeman were convinced that to follow Hutchins would amount to betrayal of the Fund's original purpose. Others, like me, were in agreement with Hutchins that a "basic issues" program was compatible with the Ford Foundation's motives in setting up the Fund.

In order to strengthen his hand with the board, and only for that reason, Hutchins sent me out on the road to sample the opinion of some of the leaders of thought. I interviewed James Reston in his Washington office. He said that the idea was a splendid one but that Hutchins' leadership was inevitably controversial and would involve even the most undebatable of principles in pros and cons. A good idea, he thought, but the abrasive Hutchins was not the man to execute it. Almost all others were enthusiastic and gave the effort a clear go-ahead. Only one professor, a philosopher at Harvard, sent in a bill for his professional opinion.

In the meantime, Adam Yarmolinski, a determined little man, was privately politicking among members of the board. The board was supposed to meet in Washington in connection with a public dinner that was given the support of Sam Rayburn and consequently attracted an unusually large number of politicos—congressmen, Supreme Court justices, and federal bureau chiefs.

At the actual meeting of the board, the cool Robert Hutchins outlined what was then called the Basic Issues program, with persuasive eloquence. Then Adam Yarmolinski rose to speak. He was earnest and sincere but no match for the charismatic Hutchins. The urbane president of the organization did not even condescend to answer Yarmolinski's arguments, but called for an immediate vote. To no one's surprise, the board voted overwhelmingly for the new plan. Some members cautioned that the findings and dialogues of the "New Founding Fathers" Hutchins had proposed to enlist for the work would have to be effectively "implemented." There was general agreement that such precautions be taken; otherwise a self-centered, Ivory Tower effort might result.

Hutchins' immediate task was to obtain the services of a group of consultants who would measure up to the ideals he had spelled out—eloquence and insight, as well as unusual intellectual training and variety, were needed. The present staff would serve as the secretarial and research assistants.

From being a conventional foundation, then, the Fund for the Republic was changed overnight into an educational institution of sorts. The need for an anti-McCarthy effort was no longer pressing. The junior senator from Wisconsin had suffered a notable decline of popularity, and Washington rumor had it that alcoholic excess was seriously influencing his health.

We were pleased by the new turn and prouder than ever of our tall, handsome leader. Of course, the defeated Adam Yarmolinski and David Freeman knew that they would be expected to turn in resignations. During the controversy, relations between them and Hutchins had so utterly deteriorated that further cooperation was out of the question.

Santa Barbara, 1971

John and Theodora with their first child, Terence, in 1943

With fellow editors of Commonweal *in New York in 1952
(left to right) William Clancy, Edward Skillin, (Cogley), and
James O'Gara*

Francis Cardinal Spellman congratulates John Cogley after he receives the Catholic Press Association's top award for his 1964 coverage of the Vatican Council.

Religion Editor of The New York Times, *1966*

CHAPTER VII

Basic Issues

THE changes at the Fund were destined to bring me back once more to the world of religion. With the first reorganization of the Fund's work, we divided the Basic Issues program into several projects. Every member of the executive staff was responsible for a project and the consultants were to integrate them all. One or two members of the board, and one or more of the consultants were assigned to each project.

Because of my background, I was the staff person put in charge of "Religious Institutions in a Free Society." The board liaisons were Dr. Henry Pitney Van Dusen, then president of Union Theological Seminary; Msgr. Francis J. Lally, editor of the Boston *Pilot*; and Eleanor Stevenson, wife of the president of Oberlin College. These people did not actually have much to do with the work, but we were delighted that the assignments to projects got members of the board directly involved in the new program.

The consultants attached to the project were both eminent theologians—Reinhold Niebuhr and John Courtney Murray, S.J. They presented a lively contrast to each other—Niebuhr folksy and instinctive, Murray classical in manner and intellect and academically, highly disciplined. Both clerics were chosen after four or five weekend meetings held at places like the Plaza Hotel in New York and the Princeton Inn in New Jersey. All who took part in these meetings were intellectually distinguished, but a few were disappointingly inarticulate. Almost every one of them, however, seemed ready to cooperate with Robert Hutchins in the new program. There were probably at least one hundred such persons tested; far too many to find a place for. A group was finally settled upon, for various reasons such as interest, articulateness, availability, age, reputation, religious or nonreligious allegiance. They included, besides Murray and Niebuhr, Henry R. Luce of *Time*; Robert Redfield, anthropologist; Scott Buchanan, philosopher; Eric Goldman, historian; Isidore Rabi, physicist; Eugene Burdick, novelist and political scientist; Clark Kerr, educator; Adolf Berle, diplomat; George N. Shuster, educator; and, of course, the Fund's own Robert M. Hutchins.

The group met officially for the first time at a meeting held at the Greenbrier, the palatial hotel which dominates White Sulphur Springs, West Virginia. The initial dialogue was about federal aid to parochial schools. Differences of opinion showed up immediately—not only on the topic in question but in the various styles of thought. Some of the consultants were philosophically pragmatic and permanently marked with the positivism they had first learned in college. Others, like Father Murray and Scott Buchanan, revealed a scholastic bent, reflecting their own training and study.

Hutchins, who said very little, was quietly suspected by several consultants of having maneuvered a Thomistic coup. The positivists at first felt that they were window dressing for a display of his Aristotelian wares, such as had caused a stir at the University of Chicago some years earlier. It was true that Hutchins had a predilection for the formalism of Aquinas. But he did nothing to deserve the reputation of being a philosophic *agent provocateur.* He was interested only in the group's reflecting the widespread pluralism which existed in the United States, in and out of the universities, and he went beyond the rigidity of campus conventionalism in drawing the boundaries.

There was a great deal of mutual criticism among the consultants, even after they had attended several meetings together. The scientific-minded among them were suspicious of the philosophers' reasoning, and vice versa. Each was a star in his own firmament and unused to the intellectual disdain that some of the leading lights of the group poured on their fellows' proposals.

Throughout, Hutchins grumbled privately about the group's inability to reach even a tolerable public cordiality, but to each member he was the essence of courtesy. To the board, he spoke encouragingly and shrewdly: that is, he was pessimistic enough to be credible. "We have a great deal yet to learn about the methods of making the most of the intellectual resources at our command," he wrote. "The pro-

cedures for the conduct of meetings, of relating the work of the projects to that of the central group, and of using outside experts can,
and I hope will, be improved."

One of the projects was my religion study, organized along the
same dialogic pattern that the program itself had established. We had
a carefuly chosen body consisting of two Roman Catholics, two
Protestants, two Jews, and two agnostics who preferred to be
called humanists.

The two Catholics were William Gorman, former editor of the
Great Books project, and William Clancy, my *Commonweal* colleague,
then working as the publications chief for the Council on Religion and
International Affairs. Gorman was militantly Aristotelian. Clancy,
more liberal, had just as deep a devotion to Roman Catholicism but
no particular affection for the Thomistic expression of its dogma.

One of the Protestants, F. Ernest Johnson, a courtly old gentleman
who was retired from the executive staff of the National Council of
Churches, was determinedly ecumenical; the other, William Lee Miller, magazine writer and professor at the Yale Divinity School, was
young, affected rustic manners, and was given to pithy aphorisms.

The Jews were Arthur Cohen, a polysyllabic young publisher who
was pioneering in paperback theology with Meridian Books, and
Rabbi Robert Gordis, a middle-aged scholar at the Jewish Theological
Seminary of America. Gordis had a shot-gun verbal delivery and
always seemed determined to discover how seeming contradictions
could be reconciled. He was the only "company man" in the group,
taking the conventional Jewish position on every conceivable subject,
while repeating ritualistically that there actually was no "Jewish
position."

Robert Lekachman, a young Columbia University economist, was
added to the group at the specific recommendation of Reinhold
Niebuhr. His companion in upholding humanism was a patrician
New Englander from the Harvard Law School: Mark De Wolfe Howe,
then in his fifties. From time to time, Dr. Niebuhr, Father Murray, or
both dropped in on our all-day meetings. We also evolved a plan for
lunching with a leader, like the chief of the American Civil Liberties
Union or the head of the Legion of Decency, to deepen our theoretical
discussions with facts.

There was, oddly enough, more dialogic discipline among this sub-
group than among the central consultants. Confessional theologies
lurked under the surface, of course, but our topics for discussion were
practical social issues—censorship by religious groups, federal aid to

parochial schools, Sunday closing laws, teaching of religion in public schools, the election of a Roman Catholic to the presidency.

Probably the most significant event the project sponsored was a week-long interfaith and no-faith gathering at New York's World Affairs Center. About a hundred religious and humanist leaders were invited. Very few declined.

That was in May, 1958. We were concerned that the Roman Catholic priests we had invited might be required to turn down our invitation, but the times were already changing. As far as we knew, none of them even asked for permission to attend. They all felt free to come to Father Murray's opening lecture, which was later included in his luminous book, *We Hold These Truths.* Roman Catholicism was, in fact, proportionately represented at the gathering. And a good thing, too. For the general subject all week was criticism and defense of Catholicism as a social force in America. The Roman Catholic Church seemed to be attacked and alternately defended out of all proportion to its place in the "four conspiracies" Father Murray had described in the opening speech—Protestantism, Roman Catholicism, Judaism, and secular humanism.

The proceedings of the conference, digested by Donald McDonald of the Davenport *Catholic Messenger*, were later published by the Fund; and the leading lectures, edited by me, were published in a widely circulated paperback, *Religion in America.* The contributors included Niebuhr, Murray, Paul Tillich, Abraham Joshua Heschel, Gustave Weigel, and others equally distinguished.

At this affair, I first heard the word "dialogue." It was proposed by Walter Ong, S.J., a disciple of Teilhard de Chardin. There was, of course, an ecumenical movement earlier, but it did not include Roman Catholics, who were even forbidden to attend general meetings at the World Congress of Churches in Evanston, Illinois, a few years earlier.

I did not attend many meetings of other Fund projects, but they seemed to be going along splendidly, according to the reports of their directors. They were all organized differently. For instance, Paul Jacobs, now in charge of labor union studies, had dozens of individual reports under way, whereas Walter Millis, a veteran newsman in charge of the study of national defense, preferred to work strictly alone.

We had early adopted what was called "the institutional approach"; that is, we chose to study actual American institutions as opposed to the Bill of Rights abstractly conceived. The idea, Hutchins' own, turned out to be very practical. We were thus able to take account of the development of education, political parties, and television, which are not even mentioned in the basic American documents. Of course, we measured the impact of these institutions in contemporary society against the canons laid down in the nation's official written goals and ideals.

When the controversial side of the Fund for the Republic was finally behind us, there was one last hurrah which involved the House Committee on Un-American Activities and me.

One day in 1957, about a year after my appearance in Washington, I received a phone call from a staff man representing the dread committee. He asked me, politely enough, for the files and names I had refused to turn over to the committee. If I quietly gave them what they were looking for, he said, the exchange would be kept confidential and no one need be the wiser. If, on the other hand, I clung to the lofty position I had taken, I would be subpoenaed again.

To accept would mean that I would be going back on the pledge given to the theatrical people who had been given every reason to believe that details of their political history would never be turned over to anyone else. I asked for twenty-four hours to consider the choice.

That evening I was at home alone; Theodora had taken the children to our country place. The proposition suggested was tempting. I had certainly found the original appearance an ordeal. However, in a moment of moral decisiveness, I put myself beyond temptation forever by burning the coveted files. I almost set the neighborhood on fire while I was at it, but I felt better for having performed the irrevocable deed. The next day I phoned to tell the staff man what I had done, and a few hours later a new subpoena-server appeared.

Now I knew that I had a public relations difficulty and I turned the problem over to the knowledgable Frank Kelly. When Kelly was originally recruited to undo Hutchins' lofty, silent indifference to the press and Ferry's noisy disdain and contempt, I asked him how he felt about his new job. He answered tersely, and typically, that he felt like a man who had just been hired to popularize the American Society for the Promotion of Leprosy. However, he cheerfully undertook the impossible.

At Kelly's suggestion, I wrote an article for *Commonweal*. He sent the article, after it was rushed into print, to a number of newspaper editors he knew personally, and to politicians he had encountered during his service as a congressional aide in Washington. The result was a rash of editorials in papers from coast to coast, castigating the committee. Not that all these editors had suddenly become enamored of the Fund. But Kelly was cunning enough to know that even a slight attack on the reporter's privilege would stimulate a lively response from them.

After this publicity, a second telegram came from Washington which postponed the threatened hearing. Then a week later a third wire postponed it further. Finally, as the scheduled hearing came close, Congressman Walter put off the hearing indefinitely. Kelly's strategy had worked.

There was no question of Robert Hutchins' creative leadership of the Fund. The Basic Issues program actually turned out to be an unusual melding of the academic and the practical. We certainly did not think of ourselves as pure academics, though we were not averse to involving academics in the work. Nor did we think of ourselves as social activists, which, in any case, was legally forbidden by our charter. Rather, we regarded ourselves as pioneering a new style of education.

In addition to my satisfaction with my new job, my home life was changed and I was content indeed with the new arrangements. The only trouble was the unconscionable amount of time I spent coming and going to and from the city. At first, I actually spent three hours on the Long Island railroad every working day.

One day, someone mentioned Brooklyn Heights very favorably. On a Sunday afternoon we traveled over there to survey the territory. We were enchanted with what we came upon—tree-lined streets, elaborate row houses built a hundred years earlier, a great promenade along the water's edge, and, added to all this, a fine mixture of races, classes, and religions. It was, of course, Brooklyn, and the mere mention of the borough always got a laugh. But we decided immediately that the only thing to do was to move there as soon as possible.

We purchased a big mansionlike house from a terminally ill doctor on Henry Street, who took such comfort in the fact that his house would be lived in by a young family that he sold it to us at far below its market value. The children went to neighborhood schools—Saint Charles Borromeo and the Friends' School. It was less than a half-hour away from the office and we were all quite content. A lifetime arrangement—so we thought.

When we had told our Long Island neighbors that we were moving—to Brooklyn of all places—they were shocked. The city and its tenements, held unhappy memories for most of them. Admittedly, both Theodora and I had our moments of uncertainty before the actual move. But the two years we spent in Brooklyn Heights turned out to be among the best in our lives.

Hutchins, trying to live contentedly in New York, was not so successful. He had one housing misfortune after another. We learned that he and Mrs. Hutchins intended to return to California and had actually purchased property in Santa Barbara. Soon we began to hear more and more talk that a busy Manhattan penthouse was no place for the kind of work we were doing; we needed a setting less hectic than the Lincoln Building, where enough people gathered every day to form a small city. Then he began to talk about the Fund establishing a permanent institution far away from Grand Central Station, although houses fit for such a purpose were easily available on the east side of New York. Finally he boldly proposed California as the place, specifically Santa Barbara, where, as we all knew, his land was located. We knew, too, that what Hutchins wanted, Hutchins usually got.

At their meeting in the Hotel Plaza in May, 1959, he told the board that he had found an estate in Santa Barbara, that it was ideal for our purposes, that it was located near a campus of the University of California, and that it was so cheap the very rich Cyrus Eaton wanted to buy the property for himself and let the Fund use it for nominal rent until its value notably increased, as it inevitably would. He had, of course, seen to it earlier that Eaton made such an offer.

The proposition won both support and objection from the board. Some said that the Fund's activities would soon lose their effectiveness if they were produced in the "cultural desert" that was California. This terminology, predictably, enraged the westerners on the board, who were immediately lined up for the Hutchins plan, particularly when he assured them that a wealthy benefactor was ready to underwrite the cost of the move. The board, of course, in old-style paternalistic fashion, never consulted the staff, though whole families were intimately involved in their decision. I remember that as the vote was taken, I whispered to Ping Ferry, "They are picking out your grandchildren." As it turned out, they actually were, Ferry's grandchildren and mine.

As expected, the vote was overwhelmingly for California. Hutchins moved fast, but carefully. There was no year-long departure from the East Coast. A few weeks sufficed. I had to put the house in Brooklyn Heights on the market immediately. With others of the staff, some secretaries included, I visited beautiful Santa Barbara. While there, I put a down payment on a large Spanish-style house, with several palm trees and a gigantic patio. The children certainly would not find here what they had grown used to in perhaps the most urban spot in the world.

REFLECTION THREE

During those first years with the Fund for the Republic, I also wrote a weekly column for Commonweal and contributed to other journals. For example, for a brief period, I wrote a weekly piece on television for the New Republic. As a Commonweal columnist, I was only a mild harbinger of the explosive Catholicism that was soon to erupt throughout the Church. I never really probed very deeply into the existing ecclesiastical order. But from some of the violent reactions that the column stirred among readers, one might conclude that I had set out to smash the barque of Peter into smithereens.

It was a transition period for Roman Catholicism. It was also one of unusual acceptance of Catholics in the United States. A universally popular pope, John XXIII, sat uncomfortably on the throne in Rome, and a youthful, Harvard-trained, old-fashioned Boston Catholic, John F. Kennedy, presided gracefully in Washington.

The changes that were soon to come about were really inevitable, but until the Second Vatican Council, the ecclesiastical authorities everywhere stoutly resisted them. Commonweal still had to be passed around surreptitiously in many religious houses and seminaries. Worship, the Benedictine review, which featured Father H. A. Reinhold's lively "Timely Tracts" and was open-minded about the use of the vernacular in the Mass and other basic changes in the liturgy, was frequently regarded as downright subversive.

After the quietude of the postwar years, there was a resurgence of lay activity. Interest in the race problem grew by leaps and bounds in the Roman Catholic community and criticism of the economic status quo was certainly not as unusual as it had traditionally been.

The active role being taken by the Catholic "new breed" was treated seriously in columns and editorials in the diocesan press. Catholic scandals, or at least some of them, were beginning to be aired freely. A young Swiss theologian, Hans Küng, received surprisingly loud applause everywhere when he traveled across the country denouncing "unfreedom" in the Roman Catholic Church. Küng called for reform and renewal during the ecumenical council that Pope John had announced would begin in Rome during the fall of 1962.

Dr. Küng drew huge crowds. I followed him on the lecture platform at St. Mary's College, Oakland, California, where agents were sent from the chancery office to tape what I said. Every dissenting word seemed to be challenged during the question period by some clerical spokesman loyal to the old order. For instance, I was defiantly asked to name even one layman, aside from

Thomas More, who had played an important part in the history of the Church. The layman's role, it seemed, was not to ask why—as I was doing—but to do and die. The Holy Ghost must have been sitting on my shoulder that night, for I answered the questioner immediately with "The Blessed Virgin Mary." There was a burst of laughter in the hall, and I realized that my flippant reply had easily carried the crowd.

However, such victories were few and far between. If the old order did not disappear overnight, it might have hung on a great deal longer without the exposure to modern. theological thought that the American bishops were confronted with during the Second Vatican Council.

The vibrant subculture that American Catholicism had erected, originally as a defense against Protestant belligerence, was still thriving. For instance, though the time had still not come when there was a forthright espousal of contraception by theologians, there was the beginning of concern because anti-birth control laws were being kept on the books in New England through Catholic pressure, even though the legislation was originally written by Comstockian Protestants (as Catholics delighted in reminding Protestants). Censorship was also letting up. The Legion of Decency, under new leadership, was valiantly trying to gain for itself a new national image as a positive force for good films rather than an inhibitory power that rewarded mediocrity. More and more Catholic names were showing up on the rolls of secular colleges, and there were priests and religious—usually alumni of non-Catholic graduate schools—who claimed not to be Thomists at all and who seriously doubted that Francis Thompson's "The Hound of Heaven" was the greatest lyric poem of modern times. Catholics no longer spent much time trying to discover whether William Shakespeare was baptized by a priest still faithful to the papacy, and practically none at all proving the death-bed conversion of George Washington. They were beginning to feel at home in the United States.

But the ecclesiastical authorities felt obliged to support the policies of the international Church, which were, of course, set mainly in Rome. Essentially, the defensive posture remained. Once, when I complained in a public speech about the lack of due process in the Church, a priest replied that with Canon Law the individual's rights were more securely protected than the citizen's rights were under the Constitution. Again, I heard a well-traveled monsignor, who knew every corner of the Church in the United States, say that, though he occasionally ran across a priest who found obligatory celibacy difficult or personally impossible, he never even heard of a cleric who did not approve of the policy itself.

Just about the time the Council was to begin, there had been a rash of articles and books focusing on "honesty in the Church," undoubtedly in-

spired in part by the work of the intrepid Hans Küng, but also by the youthful American leaders whom Father Greeley had aptly dubbed "the new breed." At the same time, Donald J. Thorman's book, The Emerging Layman, *became a Catholic best-seller. It challenged the laity, in rather pastoral language, to take a more prominent place in the Church, not particularly as helpmates of the clergy but as independent, albeit obedient, Christians.*

There were vague, somewhat timid hopes for the Council that was about to convene in Rome on October 11, 1962. There was also a good measure of cynicism that not much would come of the gathering. The old feeling persisted that "popes come and popes go, but the Curia goes on forever." The majority of American bishops were not expecting to do more than put their united blessing on the status quo.

Things turned out rather differently from what was expected. In time, timid bishops were emboldened; unchangeable bishops, who were only few in number, dug even more deeply into their entrenched ways. The actual leaders, liberal priests and laymen, did not expect that a great deal would be accomplished. Their demands were few in number. Originally they were much less radical than the Council's actual decrees—a change in liturgical practices perhaps; a lifting of outmoded fast and abstinence laws; and, in the name of ecumenism, maybe a suspension of the laws against interfaith efforts in secular affairs—that was about as far as even the most daring intended to go at first.

Cardinal Spellman, on the eve of the Vatican Council, was the actual, but widely unpopular, leader of American Roman Catholicism. He and his West Coast counterpart, Cardinal McIntyre, were solidly entrenched. The popes chose to fill the vacant sees across the country with other clerics made according to the image and likeness of men such as these. It seemed, also, that Rome acknowledged them as obedient and loyal leaders whose judgment was worth following. There was no reason, then, to hope that the forthcoming council might result in radical changes in the Church, but there was also no reason to believe that the changes it might effect would be slight, either.

I was a minimalist. I did not entertain the notion that the Church in se *was other than what Pius XII had said it was in* Mystici Corporius, *a body of true Christians who basked in the Roman certitude that they had the only full gospel and who would wait patiently for fellow Christians to see the error of their ways and "return" to papal obedience. To tell the truth, I do not think I really cared greatly. Of course, I still attended Anglican churches, breaking the disciplinary rules against participating in "false worship." Yet I thought my addiction to Episcopal worship was merely an aesthetic idiosyncracy, to be carefully hidden from others. But it was enjoyable, and the wicked secrecy it entailed heightened the pleasure.*

Of course I really did not see the reason for Roman Catholic aloofness, though I knew the arguments made for it—promiscuity in devotions was based on the idea that one form of Christian worship was as good as another, a heresy generally labeled "religious indifferentism."

I really believed that in doctrine, theological discipline, and the validity of its priestly orders, the Church of Rome was the only true Church, and that though non-Catholic Christians might surely achieve salvation, their redemption would be despite, not because of, their schismatic and heretical assemblages. Modern Protestants and Orthodox were, it seems, "invincibly ignorant." However, there was no reason why, as American citizens operating under the tolerant charter of "pluralism," we who had the full theological truth could not cooperate in the work of self-government, as Jacques Maritain kept insisting. Maritain spoke glowingly of a "charter of practical agreements" on which to base American democracy.

CHAPTER VIII

Santa Barbara

SANTA Barbara, in contrast to the busy, crowded city we had
just left, was like a continuous vacation in a wonderland by
the sea. Our new home was located near the Pacific Ocean, in lush
exurban Montecito. We actually had to get used to all the natural
beauty around us. It was not easy to adjust to the luxuriant leisure
and slow pace of the area. We were used to more hustle and bustle
and a broader variety of clashing cultures. Here, to be sure, there was
a sizable Mexican subculture, but to all outward appearances those
who lived within it were decently housed and integrated into the
economy of the area. After all, as we were to learn during the annual
fiestas the city sponsored to mark its Indian-Spanish beginnings,
those who occupied the spacious homes and remodeled mansions of
the old rich, such as the McCormicks and the Blisses, were the new-
comers, immigrants in a land where they were welcomed by the
natives for the wealth they could add to the beauty the district already
enjoyed.

The sun-seeking invaders were also responsible in no small degree
for adding to that beauty. In *Two Years Before the Mast* (1840), Richard
Dana wrote of Montecito; this now palmy area on the outskirts of
Santa Barbara was one of the most arid, bleak lands he had ever been
in. By our time, Montecito was flourishing with costly imported
beauty—trees and plants and various species of fruits and cacti from
all parts of the globe.

The result of all this, of course, was a more relaxed citizenry than we were accustomed to in New York and a less tense work force maintaining it than we had ever run across before (though the unexcitable Swiss in their orderly way had suggested the same sort of unhurried pace). In any case, Hutchins proved to be correct that under the Stars and Stripes there was a Riviera-like spot where intellectual activity could be carried on without undue distraction and with just about every modern comfort. If we desired big-city attractions, they could be found in less than a two-hour drive to Los Angeles.

The Center itself had originally been built as one of the grandest and most impressive mansions in the county. A large building surrounded by almost fifty acres of carefully tended lawns and gardens, it had been erected some forty years earlier by Frederick Cluett Peabody, the haberdasher. Later, it was inherited by his Irish-born wife, whose death, along with the almost simultaneous demise of her third husband, left the estate to be used by others in 1959. It already seemed too grand to serve as a family dwelling. With some slight alterations, however, it was easily transformed into institutional use. It became our Parthenon.

The Center for the Study of Democratic Institutions, as we called the place, at first merely expanded the Basic Issues program that we had known in New York. However, we soon began a daily dialogue among the group on the old familiar subjects, with the staff playing the role originally designed for the consultants. In addition, we brought in every well-known visitor who happened to be in Santa Barbara.

The founding fellows at the Center included Hutchins, Scott Buchanan, Frank Kelly, W. H. Ferry, Hallock Hoffman, Edward Reed (our urbane editor), and me. Reed and Buchanan both died in the nineteen sixties. Kelly, Ferry, and Hoffman later left the Center during its several reorganizations. Of course new staff members were added over the years.

The women who formed the original group, usually secretaries, found it harder than the men to adjust to the new life. That was also true of the wives who accompanied their husbands west. Everything was just too different. Some women, of course, held on to become Californians tried and true. Others, after a few weeks' effort, returned to New York or tried other places. Their jobs were frequently taken by local workers. Secretaries, it seemed, were plentiful in the Santa Barbara area.

Two new men were soon added to the staff. Harry S. Ashmore, a member of the board and former editor of the *Arkansas Gazette*, had won a Pulitzer prize for journalistic bravery during the racial strife in Little Rock in the 1950s. Ashmore, though on the Fund board, joined the rest of us as an equal under the benign direction of Robert Hutchins. Of course he did not have the New York experience behind him, and his being a trustee (as was Hutchins) caused a certain ambiguity in his role. He brought to the new Center the spirit of jovial competition that had marked his earlier jobs, a spirit which he personally (and probably quite honestly) interpreted as only a loyal concern for the welfare of the total undertaking.

From the beginning, Ashmore made a point of remaining extremely close to Hutchins, which somewhat shut out the rest of us. Ferry, the superloyal companion of the very controversial days, was conspicuously included. We soon found that the Fund, in its new incarnation, did not have the spirit of the we're-all-in-this-together camaraderie that pulled us through the bad days in New York.

Not that Ashmore was mean or ungracious to anyone. He was the embodiment of southern affability. Slowly, however, the staff's relationships with Hutchins changed. Office doors were now kept closed, and the staff had to ask Hutchins to call meetings to review the overall situation of the Center. Ashmore too insistently claimed disinterest in his own position, but the new atmosphere of bureaucratic secrecy was generally attributed to him. Rather than admitting responsibility for it, he thought it the most natural thing in the world that he should operate privately, in the manner of a representative of the board found mysteriously among the regular employees. Everyone knew, however, that he was not just one more employee. From the very beginning, he was just a little more equal. In any case, this humorous, affable southerner introduced a new element into the chemistry of the Center staff. We never again recaptured the New York innocence.

The other new addition was James V. Brady, a native Brooklynite who had become a Santa Barbara real-estate broker long before the Fund for the Republic arrived on the scene. He was obviously miscast in the role of fellow of the Center and left after a few years of futile efforts to change. He returned to his original calling, unfortunately somewhat battered by the short foundation experience. The Fund's president, in asking Brady to join the staff, had made a well-intentioned but typical misjudgment of people—a trait we were all keenly aware of. Nevertheless, Hutchins continued with more or less success to add to the staff, with barely nominal assent from others involved in the enterprise.

When we first came to Santa Barbara, we thought that in some sense we were retiring from the world. The world, though, as represented by the academics who went out West, soon found us out. At first, we merely took advantage of visitors to the Santa Barbara community. But soon invitations were issued—specialists participated in the dialogue four or five times a week. They came from all over the world. Many remained obscure figures, but I also remember visits from Arnold Toynbee, Abba Eban, Eugene McCarthy, Gunnar Myrdal, Paul Tillich, Aldous Huxley, and others of great eminence.

The tendency of the new Center was to become a straight academic institution with a flair for public relations, thanks to Frank Kelly and the imaginative Hutchins. Scott Buchanan, who joined the regulars full-time, was indisputably the academic leader. During those early years, Buchanan, a contemporary of Hutchins, wielded a mighty intellectual influence. He believed that our former direct interest in practical issues amounted to a kind of betrayal of the intellectual vocation. The Center people were justly paid for "thinking," he said, as medieval monks were supported for praying. We served the general community merely by thinking hard and long about public questions. We should not worry about what immediate effects, if any, we were having on the world. In the long run, these effects would take care of themselves.

Buchanan was a sly one who always seemed to have a secret that, with great effort, could be unearthed if an observer were percipient enough. Hutchins remarked once that Buchanan had intrigued him for thirty years by hinting at but never quite revealing the source of human wisdom. During dialogues, some hardy members of the Center, using more straightforward language, would try to sum up the insights Buchanan had just uttered. "Is that what you meant?" they would ask. And the answer was a characteristic "You *almost* have it." Then a tantalizing silence with no further explanation offered.

The charismatic Buchanan, without effort, commanded universal respect. Almost everyone loved and respected him. However, one visiting fellow, though an agnostic, put forth the theory that Scott behaved suspiciously like Satan himself: whenever clarity in a discussion was about to be reached, he sounded a note of disorder, and did so charmingly.

Scott Buchanan was far ahead of the times on most matters. Hutchins remembered that Buchanan had suggested foreign aid years before such a proposal actually reached Congress. I remember that he was a Christian believer, formally Congregationalist, who said he was on the "periphery" of the Church and was quite sure that the "center' of Christianity was in Rome. He often proposed that our religion group should drop discussions of school buses and Sunday closing laws and carry on dialogues about rigidly theological themes like grace and predestination. I was convinced that the group could only fruitfully discuss what they held in common as American citizens. Buchanan, on the contrary, felt that theological clarity might arise out of discussion of forthright ecclesiastical issues. The rest of us, carefully warned by Jacques Maritain, agreed that such a procedure would probably be disastrous.

The major denominations are now engaged in just such dialogues on theological matters as Buchanan suggested. They are finding that they were often saying the same thing in different languages or had been confusing cultural development with doctrinal requirements. Obviously, we were wrong and Buchanan quite right.

The brilliant Robert Hutchins, without trying very hard, was a nonpareil among leaders. He intrigued even Scott Buchanan. Hutchins' unfailing high style and sense of appropriateness remained unrivaled. Even when he reached his seventies, the first thing that hit one who met him was that his labors, though perhaps important for others, were really beneath those bountiful talents—that the particular job he held was unworthy of his stupendous abilities. This was true of the leadership of the Center; earlier it held for the presidency of the University of Chicago; and still earlier for the youthful deanship of the Yale Law School. The same would be true if he had reached the Supreme Court or even (an idea he toyed with as a boy) the White House. To compete with Hutchins was out of the question. The only thing left to the staff was to vie for his favor, like rival saints currying God's special concern.

There was, of course, a great deal of that sort of thing at the Center. I remember once realizing that Hutchins paradoxically cultivated a Catholic mind with a Protestant conscience. His famous predilection for the stern reasonableness of Thomas Aquinas was only skin deep, however. The true formative influence on his character was his Calvinistic father, a Presbyterian parson. He himself no longer claimed to be devoted to any branch of Christianity, though his very impatience with the inanities of popular preaching was, to me, a sign of his earnest religious search.

Hutchins was a paragon of secularized Protestant virtues in his personal life, which included among other things a cordial feeling for, and understanding of, other religious traditions. He was suspected in his University of Chicago days of being on the threshold of Roman Catholicism, because of his devotion to the rational powers of Thomas Aquinas. As I could clearly see in Santa Barbara, he was also regarded as a special friend of the Jewish community because of his courage in denouncing social evil, his shameless cultivation of the prophetic tradition, and his unfailing humanism.

As the strange union of a Catholic mind joined with a Protestant conscience, Hutchins personified a difficult combination. He would, for instance, after the manner of a Thomistic Catholic, respect anyone who made a convincing abstract syllogism. But immediately, in Protestant style, he would ask: "What do we *do* about it?" The ordinary Catholic would take the new truth primarily as something to contemplate; the ordinary Protestant would not require such an elegant indication of his duty in the first place.

Hutchins was not, of course, without fault. In fact, he ostentatiously claimed his frailty in public forums, as if by selectively admitting it, he would enhance an almost too perfect humanity. I often heard him denounce his own supposed faults before large crowds. But his real weaknesses, like his easy susceptibility to flattery, went wholly unacknowledged. Of course, some of the fellows quickly caught on to this characteristic and unblushingly poured praise on the Center's president, not only in words but by deferential agreements, silences, and other gestures that reminded him that he was, at least at first, a universally beloved leader. Admiration for what he stood for was shared by everyone on the staff, and some idealized him nearly to the point of idolatry.

We were not in Santa Barbara for very long when we became aware that many of our rich neighbors were suspicious of the Fund's real purposes. Letters appeared in the local press hinting at nameless, shameless deeds. Our beautiful property was defaced by anticommunist pranksters who regularly drew a hammer-and-sickle symbol in red paint on the private road.

In those cold war days, things were not helped at all by Ferry's inflammatory letters in the *Santa Barbara News-Press*. In one letter, he said he was not so much frightened by the spectre of Russian soldiers patrolling Santa Barbara's State Street as by the preparations being made by the United States Government for nuclear devastation. Again he would be hailed as right, if his statement had been soberly analyzed. But most of the leaders in town, caught up in anticommunism, were in no mood for sober analysis.

Ferry remained harmless but boyishly sassy in his letters and speeches. He unaccountably insulted guests of the Center (in the name of free speech) and contemptuously characterized the then unknockable J. Edgar Hoover as a mere "spy swatter," a shocking nickname that was reported from coast to coast.

At the same time, Ferry was quietly performing all kinds of acts of secret charity. He supported potential artists for extended education in Europe. He was scrupulous about acknowledging the grief and suffering of other persons, and contributed to almost every idealistic cause that tried to make this a better world or diminish the suffering in it.

In those early days of the Center there was very little or no internal difficulty, but we had a great number of external enemies. However, no matter how loud the attacks, we carried on as usual. Even the unusual was handled speedily and efficiently. For example, when half our building was mysteriously burned one weekend, we simply doubled up and quietly awaited new offices. Given our unpopularity, some of us suspected arson, but the Santa Barbara fire chief officially named an electric mishap as the reason.

Several of the original religion group came to California on sabbaticals for long stays. William Gorman was a regular for years. William Lee Miller and Rabbi Gordis each spent a year as members of the staff. Dr. Niebuhr and Father Murray paid us extended visits.

Eventually, I had a new project: "The American Character." I ran forums and national symposia on that theme, as well as individual sessions of the regular dialogue at the Center. Books and pamphlets were published under its aegis, and it was widely publicized throughout the country. Several times the essence of the interviews conducted by Donald McDonald, then the dean of the Marquette School of Journalism, hit the front page of *The New York Times* and other widely read papers.

We went along in this way until the opening of the Second Vatican Council in 1962. Pope John XXIII was presiding in Rome and John F. Kennedy ruled in the White House.

I had some part in the latter of these two circumstances. For reasons that I never quite understood, I was approached by Robert F. Kennedy and asked to join his brother's national campaign staff to specialize in church-state questions. I was to work for a division of the campaign which had the euphemistic title "Community Relations." Against the advice of Father Murray, I went to Washington for a few weeks, beginning on Labor Day, 1960.

CHAPTER IX

The Kennedy Campaign

SOME time around 1959, Senator John F. Kennedy wrote an
article for *Look* magazine. In it he said that, for the officeholder, no moral obligation transcends the duty to live up to the Constitution. This brought on a rash of editorials in the Catholic press and
in some Protestant papers, especially *Christianity and Crisis*, criticizing
Kennedy vigorously for being a rank secularist, a man who had no
genuine religious sense.

At the time, I argued in the *Commonweal* column that Senator Kennedy was correct, because he threw in the all-important words "the
officeholder." I took the position that, if a man could not conscien-
tiously live up to the oath of office he has assumed, his moral obligation was to resign; he should not try to play it both ways. This point
was later incorporated into a Kennedy speech, in which he said he
would resign if he felt required by the Constitution of the United
States to act against his conscience.

After the *Commonweal* article appeared, I received a letter from the
senator. It was nothing but a thank-you kind of note. It just said that
what I had written was his actual position. As a matter of fact, I don't
think this way of putting it had ever dawned on him until, in the
Commonweal column, he saw a way out of the bind he had gotten into
and that was being ferociously criticized by the religious press.

Earlier, I had been converted to Kennedy's candidacy by watching
him on television. I was almost ashamed to support him because I
was well known as a Roman Catholic editor who had always made a
big thing of being antisectarian. It was almost taken for granted that if

a Catholic were going to run for the presidency, I would be against him. Then one came along, a man I actually supported enthusiastically, and I found the situation embarrassing.

One day, out of the blue, I got a telephone call from Ralph Dungan, a man I did not know but who knew of me. Mr. Dungan, a Kennedy staffer, asked me if I would agree to join the senator's presidential campaign. This was almost immediately after his nomination in Los Angeles. Dungan said that the Kennedy people realized that the religious problem was going to present a real hurdle and that they had set up a branch of the campaign staff which was to deal exclusively with the "religious issue." To head the branch, they had enlisted Judge James Wine, of the National Council of Churches, assisted by a man named Art Lazell, a Presbyterian minister.

I accepted the offer after a telegram came from Robert F. Kennedy, and when I arrived in Washington, the Community Relations office had already been established. The idea was that I would stay as long as might seen necessary. I remained in Washington one month. Most of the big religious issues surfaced during that time, including the meeting called by Norman Vincent Peale—the anti-Kennedy, Protestant ministers' meeting held in the Mayflower Hotel.

Mr. Kennedy's speech to the Texas Protestant ministers was also planned and given during that fateful month. I was in Houston with Judge Wine on the day the speech was given. We went to the Rice Hotel the night before, and at breakfast we met with the representatives of the group of clergymen Kennedy was going to address in order to draw up some ground rules for the confrontation. The rules arrived at, with agreement on both sides, were that there would be no screening of questions, that the candidate would take them as they came, and from anybody in the audience. We did not think the candidate could go further than that. This was done without consultation with Kennedy or anyone on his staff.

The clergyman who headed the delegation, however, seemed worried about the fact that the Church of God people, who were among the most extreme anti-Catholics in Texas, might get on the program and thereby give Texas Protestantism a bad image. He was interested, therefore, in keeping members of the Church of God from asking questions on television. Of course we would not have been terribly unhappy had they conveyed a bigoted image. However, none of them appeared, at least not as far as we knew, on the televised part of the program.

Judge Wine and I had lunch that day with Ted Sorensen, who was not happy about the decision to have the candidate answer every question that came along. He felt that we had put Kennedy in a difficult position by reaching such an agreement. "They can ask him anything at all!" he said. "And he's on television!" Both Wine and I also became anxious about how the evening's speech was going to come off. If what Sorensen said was true, we had indeed put the candidate in a very difficult position. The die, however, was cast; there could be no changing the rules at this late hour. Sorensen said dolefully that Senator Kennedy was nervous about the speech and would certainly not be cheered up when he learned about our agreement.

Kennedy himself, however, did not appear to be at all nervous about anything, and seemed to take our decision as just one more ordeal a candidate had to go through. I threw the kind of questions at him that he would be likely to be asked. His voice was in bad shape—he was carefully saving it at the time—so he replied mostly in writing. He handed me long, lined yellow sheets of paper with his answers on them, and I kept tossing them away. Then it dawned on me that I should not be destroying these answers since this might turn out to be a historic moment. So I saved one. I still have it. It says: "It is hard for a Harvard man to answer questions in theology. My answers tonight will probably cause heartburn at Fordham and B.C. [Boston College]."

I don't remember that Wine submitted any questions. Kennedy's instant theological training was my responsibility at this particular point, and I think I covered every question that he was ultimately asked. I also presented him with some complicated questions which I was afraid he might have to face. They were, it turned out, much more sophisticated than the queries he was actually given when he went before the Texas group.

I watched the charismatic appearance in the Rice Hotel with Ted Sorensen, vaguely aware that something historic was transpiring. There were actually two audiences which Kennedy spoke to that night. One was the Protestant audience to which he talked directly; the other was the large Roman Catholic television audience "out there." He certainly did not want to say anything that would indicate to them that he had sold out his religion or betrayed the Church. He was quite aware, then, that he was walking a tightrope. In spite of this, I think his answers were honest and forthright.

After the speech, the candidate received piles of letters; all those concerned with religion, as most of his mail was, were sent to us. I do not remember how many letters arrived, but there were a great number. When we tried to find this mail later, we learned that it was destroyed or mislaid. Some of the anti-Catholic pamphlets sent to him, incidentally, were fifty years old at the time and yellow with age.

After the famous Texas speech, everything seemed to calm down somewhat. I saw no further reason to remain in Washington and came back to Santa Barbara. I wasn't really doing much at that point. The religious issue seemed to have been finally settled. Then, just about when I got back, the Puerto Rican bishops came out with their damning statement, instructing Roman Catholics on the Islands how to vote. The American controversy started up all over again. My part in that affair, however, was limited to telephone calls with Robert Kennedy, Ted Sorensen, and a few others on the campaign staff. John Kennedy simply said that the Puerto Rican affair did not affect him at all. To everybody's surprise, it didn't blow up nearly as big as everybody thought it would.

The day the Puerto Rican bishops' statement came out, everybody around the Center thought that this was the end of the Democratic line. I had to agree that they were probably right. Then, after some discussion, it was concluded that it was wisest to do nothing at all and just hope for the best. Kennedy was embarrassed by these bishops, but obviously he did not want to escalate the issue. That tactic worked out well.

Later, during the Cuban missile crisis—but not due to the crisis; it merely happened at the same time—I was appointed by President Kennedy to the Foreign Service Selection Board at the State Department, and I returned to Washington. During the hours when the Russian and American ships were approaching each other, Foggy Bottom became very tense. While I was in the conference room, I received a telephone call at the most crucial moment from a man I barely knew—Donald Michael—whom I had met casually at the Center in Santa Barbara.

The rule at the State Department for the Selection Board was that no one should be called out of the conference except for very urgent reasons. Naturally I thought that something had happened in the family. When I got to the phone, the voice turned out to be that of the last person in the world I had expected to hear from on something urgent. He said in explanation, "You are about the only Roman Catholic I know; and the only person who can do anything in this dreadful situation is Pope John. You've got to get the Pope to make a calming statement." Actually, I didn't have the faintest idea how one got a statement from the pope; privately I pooh-poohed his suggestion. I thanked Michael for his confidence in me, but added that I did not know what I could do about it.

I went restlessly through the rest of the day haunted by the idea that there must be some providential reason why I had gotten Donald Michael's telephone call. After a few hours I became almost obsessed with the notion that his idea was really a good one.

That evening when I went back to the hotel and at about 6:30 telephoned Ralph Dungan at the White House to tell him what had happened. Dungan was most encouraging. He shared the notion that such a statement would be helpful. For one thing, he said, it might get the right-wing extremists off the President's back. He also thought a statement from the pope advocating caution and urging both sides not to be carried away by nationalistic fervor might be precisely what was needed at the time. He said that he would try to do something about it. I don't know what he did, but the next morning the *Washington Post* headlined the news that Pope John XXIII had cautioned both sides to be careful, for the world's sake.

This was my first relationship with the Vatican, but there were to be others in the years immediately ahead.

REFLECTION FOUR

American Catholicism during this period made great strides toward its present ecumenical position and its "open" relationship with the world. It had not yet experienced the full force of the revolution which the innovative John XXIII unleashed later; but it had become painfully aware of its unpopular, censorious image. This image was furthered by Paul Blanshard's books, by the credence given Pius XII's supposed "vision in the garden," by the reactionary character of Humani Generis, *and by the widespread support given to Senator Joseph R. McCarthy's bogus anti-communist crusade. There were long articles and numerous letters in the Catholic press commenting on the unfavorable position of the Church in America, and much unfavorable commentary on the state of American Catholic intellectual life. Self-criticism among Catholics had already set in. The general "triumphalism" spoken of disparagingly a few years later at the Second Vatican Council was, it seemed, no longer widely accepted as a kind of fifth mark of the Church.*

The new pope, John XXIII, was still something of a mystery man. He had not yet developed into the legend he would become. All that American Catholics knew about him was that the synod he presided over in Rome was a celebration of an age they thought had long since passed. The Roman Synod did very little to meet the new problems bedeviling either the world or the Church. It was, rather, confined to such earth-shaking matters as clerical dress, the reaffirmation of the Latin language in the liturgy and in theological seminaries, and the strengthening of laws that made it even more difficult for clerics to communicate with the contemporary world.

It had already begun to dawn on many Catholics that the pontificate of Pius XII was far from a model of contemporaneity. To be a Roman Catholic, they began to see, now practically required living behind the times. And Pope John at first appeared to be carrying on in the tried-and-true mode.

For myself, I was growing more and more indifferent to the defensive measures taken by the Church. It seemed to me that there never would be a change from the stodgy Catholic manners and the legalistic interpretation with which Catholicism had obscured the Gospel of Christ.

While we were living in Brooklyn Heights I found it easy to attend Saint Anne's, an Episcopal church only a block from us, or historic Trinity Church on Wall Street, for some relief from the slap-dash liturgy at our local Roman Catholic parishes. I attended these Episcopal churches surreptitiously, of course, but found the services rewarding and dignified. Of course, I did not receive the Eucharist when the worshipers moved to the altar.

The Episcopal congregations were notably sparser than those in the crowded neighboring Roman Catholic churches. Oddly enough, though, I found I could pray better in these half-empty temples of "heresy," and I felt more at home in them than I did in churches of my own communion. I heard nothing in the articulate sermons I listened to that even slightly offended my Catholic sense of theological propriety.

Few people could help me in this difficult period. I read Protestant writers for the first time, after a lifetime of reading theology. I was impressed with the insights I found in Barth, Tillich, Niebuhr, and other Protestant theologians. Of course, I missed in them the "Catholic" sense I found in the Anglican churches I attended. I did not read much Anglican theology but only the anti-Anglican material of Cardinal Newman and the contemporary Ronald Knox. Lex orandi, lex credendi had to suffice as the principle of my Anglican instruction.

One day my old friend Father Reinhold came to town. He shared many of my feelings about the Roman Catholic Church in the United States. I told him frankly of the desire I had finally openly admitted to myself: I wanted to be an Episcopalian.

Father Reinhold understood all right, but he discouraged me from taking such a drastic step as a transfer to any other Christian Church. Individual changes, he said, no longer made sense; the ecumenical movement needed all the help it could get. I was in a position to serve the cause of Christian unity. My credibility would be in question were I to abandon the Church of my birth. Most of the Christian Churches would, of course, eventually be in communion; he was confident of that. In the meantime, one should wait until ecclesiastical leaders slowly reached some kind of bureaucratic détente.

Father Reinhold accepted the juridical primacy and even the infallibility of the pope, but he rejected Leo XIII's opinion of the invalidity of Anglican orders, pointing out that it was not an infallible statement. According to him, though I had been a disobedient son of Rome in attending Saint Anne's and Trinity, I had, in fact, participated in valid Catholic worship.

I was convinced by the Reinhold argument, and for another fourteen years I put aside any more thought of joining the Episcopal Church.

CHAPTER X

Rome

FOR the four years beginning in 1963, the city of Rome loomed
large in my life. Between the summers of 1963 and 1964, I
spent a year in Italy with my family. The following fall, with Hutchins' consent, I returned alone as a correspondent for Religious News
Service to report on the Vatican Council for the diocesan press. The
following two years I was in the Eternal City for prolonged stays as a
correspondent for *The New York Times*.

That meant, of course, that I missed the opening of the Vatican
Council and its crucial first session. Father Murray also missed it. He
confessed that he was on the original list of *periti*, the theologians
assigned to advise the bishops on the thorny issues up for discussion
in Rome; however, at the last minute, the invitation was
withdrawn—no reason given. The next year Murray was named a
peritus by Cardinal Spellman himself. He was overjoyed. "This sort of
clambake only takes place once in a man's lifetime, if he is lucky. I
would hate to miss it," he said.

No one invited us. We just went. It so happened that Robert Hutchins was not only head of the Center but chairman of the editorial
board of *Encyclopaedia Britannica*, and Harry Ashmore had in the
meantime become its editor-in-chief. In 1967 the *Encyclopaedia Britannica* was scheduled to celebrate its second centenary. To mark the
occasion, Mr. Hutchins would release three additional "perspective"
volumes. He hoped that they would "make sense" out of the mas-
sively informative articles in the regular volumes. These "roof arti-

cles" were to be concerned with science and technology, literature and the arts, the political order, mathematics, religion, among other subjects, and they were to be of book length.

Before the articles were written, their contents were laboriously discussed at the Center for over a year. They provided the focus (and the *Encyclopaedia Britannica* much of the cash) which made the Center dialogues possible during that period. When the time came for the essays to be written, Hutchins generally reached outside the Center—to Lord Ricchie-Calder, Lon Fuller, Roy McMullin, and other specialists. However, I was chosen to write the article on religion. I was so well paid that we could live frugally on the income from *Encyclopaedia Britannica* in Italy—an old dream. I knew I could attend press affairs of the ecumenical council as well.

Rome provided an exciting contrast to the bucolic placidity of our lives in Santa Barbara. We found an apartment on Monte Mario, near the Hilton Hotel, an area full of convents, religious houses, and tiny hotels.

I labored over the long article that made our *Wanderjahr* possible. I also did some work for CBS that required a few trips to London. Every weekday, as an added attraction, I attended the English-language press briefing on the theological issues of the Council.

We moved in a very international set. On Sunday evenings, the religion editor of *Time*, Robert Blair Kaiser, eager for gossip, held open house to which the Americans in town were invited. There we met all kinds of highly placed ecclesiastics and got to know the multilingual *periti*, who often did not have any language but ecclesiastical Latin in common. Archbishops were plentiful and ordinary monsignori seemed to be all over the place. Americans probably dominated at Kaiser's parties, but the varied guests also included Dutchmen, Germans, Englishmen, Irishmen, and every kind of European, as well as visitors from Latin America, India, the South Seas, Australia, and the Orient. Every now and then I would recall Murray's statement that this sort of thing occurs, at best, once in a lifetime.

I was asked to address the weekly gathering of the African bishops through the influence of Bishop Denis J. Hurley, O.M.I., an inveterate *Commonweal* reader from Durban. In the speech, I had occasion to say that, before the Council, I had known only two bishops personally in my life—Sheil and John Wright of Worcester, Massachusetts, who was later named to the Roman Curia. At that particular time the hierarchy seemed to be becoming painfully conscious of its previous aloofness, and quite undeliberately, I seemed to have struck a nerve.

The result was that thereafter strangers used to come up to me on the Roman streets and introduce themselves as Bishop so-and-so.

This was also the time when John F. Kennedy was killed. Because of our common grief, all Americans were strangely bound together, as if the tragedy could only be fully comprehended by a compatriot. However, hundreds of Italians stood in line outside the grandiose United States embassy on the Via Veneto, waiting to pay their respects to our dead President by signing a giant mourning book.

A Requiem Mass was offered for Kennedy at Santa Susanna's, the Paulist church that served as headquarters for Americans in Rome. Tremendous changes were taking place in the liturgy of the Roman Church at the time, but the old ways still held fast at Kennedy's Mass, with the result that what might have been a vibrant gathering was a staid performance witnessed by a silent, inactive congregation which had no way of expressing its grief. In a way, I suppose that this Mass marked the end of a liturgical era. But that, after all, was the Church the slain President had known all his life.

The American press panel was instructive, contentious, and colorful. Its members were usually Americans, though not always—Charles Davis, the English theologian, and the German Bernard Häring served from time to time. The usual panel included progressives like Gustave Weigel, S.J., and Barnabas Ahern, the saintly Passionist Scripture scholar, as well as such hardy conservatives as the once mighty Francis J. Connell, C.Ss.R., and his soft-spoken New Jersey supporter, Monsignor George Shea.

The purpose of the panel was to elucidate the recondite theological decisions which had been made that morning by the Council fathers. Some of the questions were frivolous and others were naïve. On the frivolous side, those directed to the unbudgeably conservative Father Connell, outnumbered the others.

Father Connell, a winsome old man then near death, had no hesitation about making strikingly concrete theological judgments. He seemed to know, for instance, precisely when a venial sin became mortal and was therefore worthy of eternal punishment. In certain economics, mortal thievery might involve $5.75; in others the venial line was held firmly at $7.65. He was certain that if aspirin were introduced into contraceptive pills, the medicine actually had to be used to cure a pounding headache or taking it would be immoral. Father Connell, despite his antediluvian theology, was unfailingly polite to his progressive questioners and consistently good-humored. He, who was once described as looking like "a debauched choir boy," seemed to be wholly admirable, even to the hypercritical Paul Blanshard. At that time, Catholic liberals thought that the ban on birth control would soon be lifted. Father Connell said that, on the contrary, the anticontraceptive teaching flowed so logically from the gospel that he would actually abandon the Church if Pope Paul ever approved "unnatural" birth control, even by silence.

Connell, if anything, was a throwback to earlier councils. Most theologians on the panel were modern, ecumenical, progressive, and eminently Bible-oriented. They were hardly surprised by Father Connell's reactions. They did everything in their power, however, to counteract the idea that their Church was forever Tridentine.

It seemed to me that some of these men held on tenaciously to old seminary formulae only by giving them entirely new meanings. They were unwilling to throw out the formula as mistaken in the first place but, rather, thought it capable of being "developed" into something quite different. For instance, "No salvation outside the Church" could be developed into "possible salvation for everyone." The original words, though now understood in a wholly new way, were kept intact. "Error has no rights," the justification for religious disabilities, was developed into the decree on religious liberty—the practical antithesis of the earlier teaching.

I certainly did not reject Newman's "development" out of hand. I even regarded a certain kind of "development" as flowing inevitably from scriptural truth. Thus, it was no great step to conclude that Jesus Christ was wholly man, given the biblical account of his birth. But to conclude as historical fact, for instance, that Mary's body was assumed into heaven, as Pius XII decreed in 1950, simply did not, it seemed to me, follow from anything in Scripture. I began to doubt then, not "development" *per se* but the ease with which the term was being used in Rome.

What surprised almost everyone at the Council was the casualness with which the fathers seemed to adopt the theology that many of them had solemnly anathematized very shortly before. This was due in part to the presence of the Eastern Uniate patriarchs. As usual in such gatherings, the pope was immune from any personal criticism. Paul VI's hesitations and fatal delays were always laid at the feet of his curial aides.

These Roman prelates, assisted by some foreigners, were particularly eager that, in the fathers' enthusiasm for "collegiality"—the idea that all Roman Catholic bishops, with the pope presiding, are responsible for the entire Church—the absolute primacy of the pope was not endangered. They insisted (to the point of ludicrousness, some of us felt) that the decree affirming episcopal collegiality must underscore the pontiff's pivotal role.

For years, I had concerned myself with the effects of different faith groups coexisting in the same society. Vatican II, in contrast, got down to abstract fundamentals. Consequently, I found it highly instructive. I had always been taught, for instance, that there was only one true Church. Now I learned that the Church Christ had founded did not exist solely as the Church of Rome, though it *subsisted* therein, in plenitude; but that there were also ecclesial elements in Protestant and Anglican bodies. For the first time in Roman Catholic official literature, these latter were described as Churches.

The word "Church" had long been applied to the Eastern Orthodox bodies (which were described as "Churches in schism"), but now it was applied also to organized groups of Western heretics. Such a use might have shocked Newman. I thought however that it was an ecumenical step of some significance. Roman Catholics still enjoyed the whole thing, of course, but other Christians shared *some* of the plenitude.

The two big issues of the Council, the schema on religious liberty and the one on the Jews, did not excite me very much, though they were popularly known as the "American" schemata because of the universal support given to them by clerics from the United States. I thought that the outcome would not affect the homeland very much.

Later, in Spain, I was to attend a Baptist clerical gathering which had to be held without publicity, behind closed doors. I realized then that there were still places where the conclusions the Council fathers reached about religious liberty were very practical indeed. Of course, we were all shocked by some of the Hitler-like judgments on the Jews pronounced in the *aula* by bishops from the Middle East.

For reasons which I will never fathom, there were people who would have liked the Council to decree a new dogma concerning the Mother of Christ. It turned out that that over-titled lady was in fact given one more name, "Mother of the Church," a harmless enough pietism of Paul VI. But why anyone would want to increase the wonder with which Mary was already supposedly endowed, lifting the greatest of the Saints even more out of the normal range of humanity, baffled me. Still, I knew that there was a zealous group anxious for Mary to be named Mediatrix of All Graces—a prerogative easy to misunderstand in a religion that holds Jesus Christ to be the unique Savior of mankind. However, because Pope John XXIII made it clear that the Council should neither anathematize evils nor declare new dogmas of the faith, those who opposed such a definition were finally victorious.

My various stays in Rome were heavily ecclesiastical when the Council was in session. During the off months though, Rome was about as secular as any other European city. Now and then I was invited to diplomatic lunches held at the American embassy. And we made friends among permanent residents in the city.

The Italian citizenry seemed to accept the ecclesiasticism of Rome with aplomb, and certainly with no sign of untoward piety; rather, they spoke of the Church as a power center, with cardinals and curial bishops influential enough to arrange for jobs, float important loans, and arrange for lucrative excursions to Italy.

For two of my three sessions at the Council, I stayed at a *pensione* about three blocks from the Vatican. Signorina Maria, the proprietress, was delighted that her rooms were constantly occupied. However, as far as I knew, she never once bothered to walk over to San Pietro's in order to see the splendid sight when 2,300 bishops were dismissed for lunch. She was indifferent to such matters. The pageantry of the Church did not impress her at all. She had the vague idea that the Church of Christ was Roman and Catholic, and that all other Christians throughout the world were simply heretics. Before the Council she was convinced that priests outside Italy were able to marry, but that the Italian clergy were forced to rely on street girls, and regularly did. When a group of youthful, vigorous, and thoroughly modern American Paulist Fathers moved into her *pensione*, she decided that it might be possible that clerical celibacy was really enforced in the United States.

Signorina Maria was a typical Roman. She did not attend Mass very often, but when she did, it was with great fervor. She considered it something of a waste of time to worry about theological matters, yet she accepted the latest dogma of the Church as unquestioningly as she believed in the existence of a divine being. God and the Church: their ways were mysterious. The Church as she knew it peopled her world with wonders: the story of Christ, the miracles still wrought by the intercession of Mary, the legends of the saints. In the meantime, the local clergy with their stylized piety were characters in a supernatural world that softened her harsh, lonely life.

This was quite a difference from the hardheaded, take-it-or-leave-it

Catholicism that most of us had known in America. In Italy, Catholicism infused the prevailing culture as well as the religion of the people. Even Italians who "outgrew" the faith continued to participate in Catholic culture.

"We make the faith and you believe it." "There is no God and Mary is his mother." "I am an atheist, but a *Catholic* atheist." These were common sayings. But through the centuries the religion of Rome was a source of local prosperity, and the realistic Italians were much too anti-ideological to dispense with it or even to acknowledge their own lack of belief—or, as seemed more likely, their half-belief.

I think the Romans were rather surprised during the Vatican Council to come up against so many foreign clerics who were quite adapted to contemporary life and yet took Christianity seriously. They regarded as quite admirable the young nuns and priests from abroad who were so very different from the clergy they had known.

A calling to the religious life in Italy usually meant a kind of prolonged childhood. Some of the local sisters seemed as innocent as babes, and the friars were not much better. However, there was a clerical upper caste gathered from all over the country, with Italianized foreign recruits to complement their company, who were extraordinarily worldly wise and (in a special sense) highly sophisticated. These belonged to the pope's own cadre, the Curia. They manipulated the faith of others and made and unmade Catholic marriages with finesse. The Curia maintained its own special cultural world. Most of its members accepted themselves as "holy men," set apart from others, not particularly for service but for the Church's own prestige.

They were lavish in handing out titles and keenly appreciated how much these distinctions meant to others. One American priest I knew who was stationed in Rome did dull, routine work that no one else wanted to tackle. Every time he threatened to return to the United States (where he might have been given one of the higher posts in his religious order) he was presented with another Vatican medal. That kind of recognition was enough to keep him going for another year.

The pope was not merely the first bishop in the worldwide Church, he was the chief of the College of Bishops, which did not even exist without him as its head. He had the power to name bishops, to interfere in the affairs of remote dioceses, to summon and to close ecumenical councils, and, if he were so inspired, to proclaim new Christian dogmas infallibly—dogmas which were "developed" from the ancient Scriptures or included in the venerable tradition of the

Church. These dogmas would then be part of the deposit of faith as surely as the Redemption itself. Of course disciplinary matters, like the celibacy of the clergy and the traditional fasts, were completely in his hands. The pontiff's was a lonely peak of eminence. It really was something of a wonder that Pope John XXIII had stayed as humble as he did and that Paul VI seemed so unsure of himself.

For the first time I began to concern myself with the stupendous claims made for the papacy. I could easily see the need for an overseer of the whole Church, a bishop who would concern himself exclusively with the Church universal. As bishop, the pope was sacramentally no more or less than other bishops. His office was not exalted by a special sacramental rite. In questions of jurisdiction, though, he was clearly superior to other prelates. He was also superior in that he alone could speak for the entire hierarchy; although by 1964, it seemed unlikely that he would ever again proclaim a dogma of the Church outside of an ecumenical council.

All in all, the declaration of papal infallibility, declared during the first Vatican Council, turned out to be pretty much an empty box. Only a very few Roman Catholic dogmas were declared via the new infallibility route and they were largely irrelevant to daily life—the Assumption of Mary, for instance, could simply be ignored.

Still, that the pope alone should be given the powers of infallibility enjoyed by the Church itself, was still something of an issue. And I began to find it disturbing that the pope was not named by the other bishops but staked his claim on the fact that he was the Bishop of Rome, chosen by the cardinals, the titular clergy of certain Roman parishes and suburban dioceses.

I would not have minded if the distinctions of the Bishop of Rome were merely honorific, but they were clearly more. They amounted to ultimate juridical power, not to be checked this side of heaven. They were symbolized in Rome by the dozens of priests we saw every day scurrying off to their curial offices. They were symbolized also by the elaborate deference paid to the supposed successor of St. Peter, who uncomfortably accepted the honors paid him as the "Vicar of Christ on Earth."

I had nothing but admiration for Giovanni Montini, the man. In private audiences and on an airplane trip with him to New York for his visit to the United Nations, he struck me as an unassuming person, solemnly convinced of the legend he embodied and truly concerned about the fate of the world.

From very early days he was destined for the priesthood. He took celibacy as a sublime part of his vocation. He was certainly no villain, but he was, I began to think, the inheritor of a historic power scheme developed by an early occupant of the see of Rome and sanctified by history.

This feeling was part of my move toward the Anglican interpretation of Christianity. I also found the Roman exclusivity arrogant and quite unbearable. At the same time, I refused to accept the earlier idea that Protestants might not be ecclesiastically Christian. Nor did I find any comfort in the platonic notion found in Protestantism, that a united Church existed in the mind of God but nowhere else. The Western Church was clearly divided; there was no blinking at that fact.

About this time, the Mass itself was changed from a passive sacrificial rite, priestly and impersonal, to a modern *agape* wherein good fellowship was rife and people marched to the Communion rail singing Bob Dylan's "Blowin' in the Wind." Father De Pauw branded these modern eucharistic celebrations "hootenanny Masses"—not without reason.

It was clear to the most obtuse, moreover, that Rome had finally given in on several points that were vibrantly controverted during the Reformation. It granted the Cup to the laity on certain occasions. It allowed the diaconate to mature married men, going at least part way on clerical celibacy. It downgraded the Index of Forbidden Books and the lists of proscribed movies. It encouraged ecumenical religious services. In some places, Catholic churchmen became very active in the local Council of Churches. It was no longer rare to hear a Protestant preacher speaking from a Catholic pulpit, and vice versa. In college settings, chaplains of every variety of Christian faith began to see themselves in a cooperative ministry, rather than as agents of rival establishments. Clerical clothes, for both priests and nuns, at first modified and modernized, began to disappear altogether. It was no longer required for the sisters to travel in pairs. House Masses were very much in vogue. Sometimes the celebrants took extreme liberties with the prescribed rubrics.

Roman Catholics found their new freedom so exhilarating that some simply left all their old religious customs behind them and began a conventionally secular way of life. The laity left the Church in about the same proportion as their formal leaders abandoned the religious life or the rectory. The number of children in American Roman Catholic schools decreased by about one million. Once popular publications dwindled in circulation and some of the most significant died altogether.

Were the changes brought on by such influential new theologians as Hans Küng and Gregory Baum? To a degree I suppose men like these scholars might be held responsible. They had broken the spell the besieged fathers of Trent had cast over Roman Catholicism. But even if such scholars had not appeared on the scene, the Church would not have been spared the upheaval. Others would have taken their place. To blame them personally was like blaming Pope John XXIII for summoning the Vatican Council in the first place.

As late as 1966 Pope Paul VI put the seal of his authoritative approval on transubstantiation—an antiquated Aristotelian notion of physics, as Father John McKenzie puts it in the new *Encyclopaedia Britannica*. Pope Paul, I know, believes in the "Real Presence" of Jesus Christ in the Eucharist, but so do many other churchmen. I was unhappy that he still made belief in the "substance" idea an object of faith. Four hundred years ago, Queen Elizabeth is supposed to have said: "His was the Word that spake it / And what His word did make It / That I believe and take it." It neatly sums up my own view.

I was really no longer a Roman Catholic in the old understanding of the term. There were, of course, many other Catholics who thought as I did and held that, according to the new theology, they were still in good standing in the postconciliar Church, because it no longer demanded their full agreement. They seemed to put forth the thesis that even Roman Catholicism itself did not take its old dogmas very seriously.

Again I was convinced that I should stay where I was. Maybe I belonged with this new type. I finally decided not to take such things so seriously; to relax and see how the furor in Roman Catholicism would end up.

REFLECTION FIVE

The mid-sixties was a very special time for American Catholics. Friday abstinence, for instance, was abolished. Only a few months earlier an article putting forth the suggestion that deliberately eating meat on Friday did not lead to eternal damnation was noted prominently in the news that The New York Times *found fit to print that day. The leaders of the fishing industry were very upset by this practical application of conciliar theology. The* Times, *I know, received letters from public relations men expressing amazement that the bishops in Rome would approve of the eating of flesh meat seven days a week.*

There were numerous opinion surveys showing that the two subjects deemed too delicate to be discussed in St. Peter's—birth control and clerical celibacy—were on the minds of a significant number of Catholics. At first—in pre-Vatican II fashion—the opinion polls were dismissed as greatly exaggerated; but as thousands of religious and priests proved them out by leaving convents and rectories to marry, the denials became notably fewer.

It was assumed that Pope Paul VI would have a hard time reversing the Catholic position on birth control. Those of us who were in Rome during the Council remember the fictitious first sentence of some future papal encyclical that Robert McAfee Brown, the Presbyterian theologian, had proposed: "As the Church has always taught, the control of population by human invention is a moral obligation." It was taken for granted that Paul would issue some kind of statement reflecting the general opinion expressed at the Council. Many priests were already advising their parishioners to go ahead with contraception.

"I am Peter," Paul VI told visitors. He was clearly convinced that, being pope, he alone had inherited Peter's office—an office greatly expanded from the days when the apostle himself led the fledgling Church. The papacy was no longer regarded as a man-made institution at the service of the whole Church; the Bishop of Rome, at least since medieval times, was formally believed to be the divinely ordained ruler of all Christians. Ecclesial bodies did not even exist in divine plenitude unless they were in communion with him. He was not only the head of the College of Bishops, but theoretically, he could personally act as the whole College. Bishops who rejected his authority were not members of the College—though their priestly orders, even in the mind of Rome, might be unquestionably valid, as was true of the Orthodox.

I knew that all this could be rationalized ecumenically by careful reasoning, but I preferred not to think very often about the case against the stupendous

Roman claims that the servus servorum Dei *should become the* magister ecclesiae *against the wishes of much of the Church.*

I knew before the argument started that the best syllogistic case in the world would never convince me that the Protestant observers who came to Rome were not truly Christian. And if they were indeed Christians, I could not see how their beliefs disqualified them from being members of Christ's Church.

I certainly was not attracted to Anglicanism in order to excommunicate Roman Catholics. I was attracted to the Episcopal Church because, except for some extremists within its body, it recognized all of Christ's baptized followers in the assemblage (ecclesia) of his own founding and yet allowed them the widest freedom of interpretation of Revelation (in accordance with the insights of the Reformers, for instance, or in the light of later secular developments).

All these thoughts crossed my mind during the time in Rome. Still, I was so thoroughly plunged into the Roman Catholic milieu I did not give them prolonged consideration. The Church I had grown up in, energized by the Council, was being transformed before my eyes.

The articles of faith that had earlier worried me were being given new meanings by progressive theologians. I was delighted, of course, that the long cold war between the branches of Western Christianity also seemed to be thawing out. More and more, we were discovering that the differences created by our ancient arguments were, when properly interpreted, largely nonexistent. Roman Catholic teaching was no longer so sectarian or defensive as it had been; it seemed that we might finally develop a genuine, modestly stated ecumenical theology as a result of this Council.

The pope himself went a long way toward that goal by publicly shouldering a proportionate Roman blame for Christian disunity. One day, for instance, he participated in a Christian interfaith service in a Roman basilica. As for the periti at the Council, they were busy signing contracts with non-Catholic theological schools at home and arranging for Protestant scholars to join their own faculties.

Nevertheless, I turned more and more to Anglicanism. It enjoyed antiquity, it claimed apostolic succession, it avoided nonbiblical superstitions, it admitted historic errors, it did not propose outmoded explanations (substantiation) for the mysteries of the faith, and it allowed for real weight in the authority possessed by all its members, lay or clerical. Moreover, contemporary Anglicanism provided for a theological pluralism that ranged from the profound conservatism of an E. M. Mascall to the progressive excesses of a Bishop Pike. This, plus the beautiful liturgy of the Book of Common Prayer, had a growing appeal for me.

The Roman arguments against the Church of England, of course, were *formidable. First of all, it was claimed that the Church of England was a highly nationalistic body, having its distinct origins in the turmoil that followed upon Henry VIII's being refused an annulment. That argument did not cut very deep with me. The pope, in Henry's time was clearly moved by political considerations alone. And I could see that sacramental marriages for people much lower than kings were casuistically nullified in twentieth-century Rome. In the meantime, the Anglican communion of Churches now included men and women of many nationalities and all races. Moreover, Henry VIII or Elizabeth did not merely establish an artificial Church in England but began with the one that was already there.*

The Church of Rome had often missionized other lands. Thus, Saint Augustine of Canterbury had been sent to England by Gregory the Great. There was no reason in my mind why Ecclesia Anglicana *should not in turn plant the Church of Christ wherever British influence was felt. The Church of England had done precisely that, finally leaving the new Church to determine its own polity.*

As far as priestly orders went, Pope Leo XIII declared in 1884 that the Anglican ordinal used in the ordination of Matthew Parker was defective in sacrificial empowerment. Parker's consecrators, he said, really had no intention of ordaining a sacrificing bishop. His ordination to the episcopate, therefore, was null and void. Anglican ordinations, no matter how many validly ordained bishops from other Churches might share in the imposition of hands, have been null and void ever since, because of the defective ordinal used. I know that Leo's opinion was not considered even by him to be infallible—but he did say it was "irreversible."

For my own part, I shared the sentiments later expressed by the Jesuit writer Edward P. Echlin, the author of The Anglican Eucharist in Ecumenical Perspective *(The Seabury Press, 1968). Echlin wrote:*

First, it seems to us that the question will never be settled with absolute certainty. The ways of God and the intentions of men are too inscrutable for such certitude. Second, there is a respectable opinion in Catholic theology that Anglican Orders are indeed valid. One cogent argument often used is the working of the Spirit in the Church. Who is to say the Spirit will be frustrated by the lack of signification of a book?

A great deal, I knew, also hinged on the meaning given to "substance" and "sacrifice" in the fourteenth century.

When I finally left Rome at the end of the Council, I was enthusiastic about developments in the Roman Catholic Church. There was good reason to be optimistic, and I looked forward to the years ahead as an era of Christian reunion.

CHAPTER XI

The New York Times

IN Rome, I heard rumors that *The New York Times* was interested in my filling a new post on the paper—religious news editor. I was not surprised, then, to be asked to stop by the *Times* office to see Abe Rosenthal (later managing editor) on my way back from the Council in 1964, for what turned out to be a job interview.

The *Times* had not previously ignored Church affairs. George Dugan, its special religion reporter, had followed clerical moves and denominational conventions for years. But the new position the editors had in mind was to be larger in scope and broader in coverage than Dugan's. Theological issues were to reported and discussed, and religion was to be handled with at least the seriousness with which the paper treated sports, education, and the theater.

The man chosen for the job would be named an editor of the paper rather than merely a specialized reporter. His work would cover all departments of the giant *Times* enterprise—the daily paper, the Sunday magazine, even the special weekly travel section. He might, for instance, be called upon to write an occasional editorial and he would be expected to go on reporting assignments anywhere in the world.

Mr. Rosenthal thought that, on the basis of the theological reporting I had done for Religious News Service (for which I later received the annual Catholic Press Association Award), I might qualify. Of course the paper would look further, and the *Times* editors wanted, in addition to my experience, to have some sort of insight into my personality.

I was excited at the prospect of the job. In the journalistic world, being an editor of the *Times* is just about as high as there is to go. The feeling I had was similar to one I had earlier, when I was first recruited by *Commonweal*.

I was not back home very long when I received an affirmative reply from the *Times*. I had made it, and at a salary considerably higher than the one I was getting. Thus, we made our move from Santa Barbara back to New York in 1965, and I became an editor of the *Times*, a position of some influence. I was convinced of that when I found awaiting me at the *Times* a letter of congratulations from none other than the Reverend Dr. Billy Graham.

I was aware that the publisher, Arthur Ochs Sulzberger, was being criticized for having the temerity to hire a well-known Roman Catholic. He was kind enough not to mention these criticisms to me, but word about them inevitably got around. I was told that my appointment was even more remarkable than the election of a Boston Irishman.

I had two assistants who both did pretty much as they pleased; they were subordinates, but only technically. One was the veteran religion reporter, George Dugan, who had extensive experience with denominational politicking and who generously taught me what he knew so well. The other was a former copyboy I had picked out to work on the religion desk because he showed extraordinarily intelligent interest in theological matters. He was, I learned later, Edward B. Fiske, a young Presbyterian clergyman.

Fiske and I left most of the conventional reporting on ecclesiastical and synagogue affairs to the seasoned Dugan and the *Times'* Jewish expert, Irving Spiegel. We concentrated, rather, on recent developments in theological thought and liturgical changes in the Churches.

For instance, it was Ted Fiske—an inveterate reader of obscure theological quarterlies—who suggested that the *Times* feature a series on "Death-of-God" theology, then barely known to the public. He then spent weeks interviewing the leading proponents of the movement and reading their work, measuring their teachings against his own academic background at Princeton Theological Seminary. Unfortunately, he delayed too long in its preparation; after the article was finally written, the *Times* went on strike. In the meantime, *Time* magazine colorfully featured "Is God Dead?" on its cover. It seemed that Fiske's pioneering work was in vain, but it can certainly be said that no religious story was ever more thoroughly or more intelligently researched than his original piece on the "Death-of-God" theologians.

My experience with *The New York Times* included service at both the frantically busy Forty-third Street office and various one-room bureaus in Europe, where life was notably less hectic. The headquarters in Manhattan were, of course, the center of the operation, where the work done around the globe was pulled together and daily integrated into "All the news that's fit to print."

The reporters' desks in the *Times'* massive home city room were placed according to their occupants' skill and industry—not by any formal election, but by an unspoken general consensus. A few old-timers, whose stories on the battles of World War II had moved millions, were now waiting for retirement and were placed with the untried rookies in the extreme rear. The older men spent most of the day playing cards or simply gossiping. They were rarely given an assignment; weeks went by without their by-lines appearing in the paper. But, of course, they clung to their jobs until that bittersweet retirement birthday arrived.

Neither the soon-to-be-retired nor the neophytes were often found in foreign correspondence. All foreign bureau chiefs were considered to be winners in the *Times'* competition. As a *Times* man, along with the reporter from *Time* magazine, the foreign correspondent also ranked informally with the American ambassador as a representative of the United States.

Everyone on Forty-third Street, and indeed in *Times* bureaus throughout the world, was sold on the paper's significance. A few of the younger reporters, of course, were pursuaded that the paper's vaunted "objectivity" was only an occupational illusion. The impact of the "new journalism" was already being felt. But the chief editors, though not adverse to making attempts at modernization, were still wedded to the old ideal. Even slight transformations did not go down well with veteran *Times* hands. For instance, some felt quite let down after learning that the paper would no longer publish the full texts of diplomatic notes on minor matters between minor heads of states. "The *Times* should be written for history," said one veteran staffer. "Who cares if living readers find this sort of thing boring?"

During my stay with the paper, the publisher and chief editors became aware that their past coverage of religion had been dull and uninspired. Vatican II became, perhaps, the most exhaustively reported event in the history of religion; and the generous space the

Times gave to it served as an infectious example to other publications. Certainly any event to which the good, grey lady of Forty-third Street gave so much attention must be worthy of public concern.

If there was any suppressive mischief at the *Times*, it was not because of conspiracy but, rather, conventional caution. Zealotry was suspect as being unbecoming a true journalist; this bias, of course, played into the hands of conventional party-liners and the manipulators of staged events. Vietnam, for instance, might have been less "objectively" reported in the interests of humanity, but the feeling at the paper then was that the purveyors of power were presumed to be right and that their formal statements and official silences only served in the national interest. Perhaps the Watergate revelations changed this attitude.

I am sometimes asked if there was undue pressure by religious groups to control the news at the *Times*. There was practically no overt effort, especially by Roman Catholics (whose record before Vatican II was not supposed to be very good in such matters). There were occasional attempts by ecclesiastical leaders to keep certain measures secret or to block the full reporting of them—this was true across the interfaith board—but in only a few cases did religious leaders threaten to use the economic power they controlled.

During this time, I had a number of attacks of angina, due to a high blood pressure condition that I had developed. One night, at a particularly tense time—strikes had severely limited the city's public transportation—I was required to walk the forty-odd blocks home from the *Times* building to our apartment on East Eighty-first Street. The weather was well below freezing and the angina grew severe. I was exhausted by the time I reached the apartment. Later that evening I suffered a mild heart attack and was soon established at Montefiore Hospital in the Bronx. The editors of the *Times* were very understanding. When I was well enough to return to work, the paper's medical staff was extraordinarily solicitous about my progress.

In the summer of 1966—after our son Terence had been graduated from Harvard, married, and gone off to India with the Peace Corps—we decided to spend our vacation in Santa Barbara. We knew many people there and the summers were remarkably pleasant. As it turned out, Santa Barbara provided a delightful contrast to the crowds and heat of New York. I was immensely pleased when Robert Hutchins asked me to return to the Center as a regular staff man.

Only the day before, a Santa Barbara doctor had told me that if I kept up the pace expected of me in New York, I would, surely have more serious cardiac trouble ahead. The quiet serenity of the Center offered a tempting alternative.

No decision was reached by the time we left, but the idea was certainly implanted in my head. I knew that I was supposed to go to Germany in the fall to cover a fundamentalists world congress. I also had an agreement with the *Times* that I would continue from Berlin on a long trip, to report on religion throughout Europe. I felt that I should honor these commitments before giving Hutchins a final reply. As Theodora and I weighed the pros and cons of the move back to California, my health was the prime consideration. Finally, I called Hutchins with a positive answer. He seemed pleased. The Center, he said, was going to put out a regular magazine, and I would be named its first editor.

The "powers that be" at the *Times* could not have been kinder. Clifton Daniel, the managing editor, replied in writing: "You brought new distinction to the columns of *The New York Times*—the kind of distinction we are trying to achieve in every area of news and commentary. It will be difficult indeed to replace you." Turner Catledge, then executive editor, wrote: "I am sure that for many years to come we will regard our coverage of the Council as an outstanding job of intelligent, thorough, and sustained reporting of a great historical event. You had a mighty part in it." Arthur Ochs Sulzberger sent a final complimentary note, adding $1500 as a practical sign of gratitude.

Just as in Europe I had been charmed by the antiquity but longed for the conveniences of modern America, so in the United States my idle thoughts turned lovingly westward. I would, of course, be sorry to leave the *Times* and old friends in the East. I had to admit, though, that I was not at all unhappy about returning to the paradisal spot that Robert Hutchins had discovered along the shores of the Pacific.

REFLECTION SIX

I had read books and listened to lectures, especially during the radical sixties, which suggested that the press was a kind of conspiracy designed to serve corporate interests. I certainly did not wholly agree, but from my experience at The New York Times, *I am now convinced that the conspiratorial case is not without foundation.*

The reason is not wickedness or selfish interest; it is, rather, a lack of imagination, fortified by highly conventional attitudes on the part of editors. New ideas always have a hard time gaining acceptance. The popular press does not envision itself as an instigator of new thought so much as a purveyor of the facts about the tried and true. No respectable publisher actually gives orders that his staff should follow this pattern; it is not usually necessary, in any case.

Once, at a Center meeting, Henry R. Luce stated unequivocally that in his long years with Time, *he had never ordered a writer to treat a story any special way. Several of Luce's fellow consultants who took a dim view of his publications' effects on American governmental policies were inclined to accept the truth of his statement. They knew it was not required by the editor-publisher that* Time *or* Life *stories be written with a certain bias. In the first place, the writer would probably be in sympathy with the general Luce position, or at least he would certainly not be antagonistic to it. In the second place, the employee would make it a point not to veer from what he divined to be the publisher's predilections if he wanted Luce's favor.*

Those who were passionately out of sympathy, for whatever reason, with the publisher's prejudices, actually found working on Luce's publications excruciatingly painful. There were such people, as there are everywhere, on The New York Times *staff, eager to practice what was being called "free journalism." "Free journalism" meant that the facts would be so presented (or suppressed) that their writing could be used primarily to serve not informative but moral purposes.*

The fact that a newspaperman has strong personal opinions, left or right, does not necessarily handicap him. A good reporter may actually be more fair than an indifferentist, if only because he is keenly aware of his convictions and knows that, seen with a prejudiced eye, the truth is easily distorted.

It was my impression that, in this sense, The New York Times *tried to be objective, though it did not always transcend the frailties of human nature. We were quite aware of the publication's weaknesses but were convinced that it was more successful than most in avoiding distortions of facts.*

To a great extent, this was due to the family traditions of its young publisher. Undramatically, he upheld the heritage of the Sulzbergers. On one occasion, for instance, a group from an important religious sect came to call on him to complain about the supposed bias of the Times' correspondent in their area of the country. They brought with them their own public relations man who suggested that, if the paper did not withhold certain racist facts about the Church's doctrines, a number of the Times' advertisers would withdraw their accounts. "Punch" Sulzberger treated the subtly worded threat with sheer disdain. "We'd lose a million dollars a year, you say? Well, thank God we can afford it."

CHAPTER XII

The Center Again

WHEN I returned in 1967 to rejoin the fellowship and begin *The Center Magazine*, I soon realized that the routines of the Center had changed. For one thing, the staff was larger, more cumbersome, and much more distinguished. Rexford G. Tugwell, the old New Dealer; Linus Pauling, the Nobel Prize winner; and James Pike, the controversial Episcopal bishop, had been added to the old staff. The discussions and dialogue sessions had become much more formal. The spirit was notably more academic, and the subjects treated were more esoteric.

Bishop Pike flew around the United States for lectures and sermons almost every week, but he prepared scrupulously for Center meetings. When the dialogue was in session, he sat reading his voluminous correspondence throughout the visitor's introductory presentation, seemingly ignoring what was being said. Actually, as he proved later by asking shrewd questions or making salient points, he had noted every word. He was an extremely nervous man and a very heavy smoker. Unaccountably, one day he gave up the tobacco habit as undramatically as he had earlier forsworn alcohol.

For the first time, others at the Center besides Robert M. Hutchins were being regularly publicized. It even reached the point where the institution became known as "Pauling's Place" or "Pike's Peak." Within the walls, however, Robert M. Hutchins remained firmly in charge.

The Center was in a prosperous period, thanks to the constant

110

benefactions and final bequests of Chester Carlson, the inventor of Xerox. Its finances were stable enough to organize another peace conference, this one in Geneva; the second such meeting to be called *Pacem in Terris*, in memory of Pope John's significant last encyclical. Geneva was chosen because Bernard Cornfeld, the notorious financier, had his home there and promised to contribute heavily.

The first of the PIT meetings had been held in New York early in 1965. This European one was to involve hundreds of international leaders, among them Martin Luther King, Pietro Nenni, and Dom Halder-Camara. Of course, the regular corps of Center fellows was also invited. So it was that I again found myself in Europe in May, 1967.

Maybe the most fiery speech delivered to this star-studded international audience was by a young Anglican prelate, Bishop C. Edward Crowther. Bishop Crowther, an Oxford lawyer turned clergyman, had been a chaplain at the University of California in Los Angeles before his election to head the diocese of Kimberly, South Africa. When he returned to his diocese after a brilliant attack on *apartheid* at Geneva, Crowther, alighting from the airplane, was formally given a deportation notice. He was ordered to get his family out of South Africa immediately. The outspoken cleric had no choice but to obey at once. Through Pike's interest in the case, the Crowthers finally wound up in Santa Barbara, where the bishop and his wife became personal friends of ours and remain so still.

This, of course, was creating another tie between me and Anglicanism, as were my membership as an ecumenical recruit on the board of the (Episcopal) Church Society for College Work and my long membership on the interfaith board of the Council on Religion and International Affairs. These relationships of course, were not the slightest bit proselytizing. I was merely accepted there by Protestant, Jewish, and uncommitted colleagues as an ecumenical-minded Roman Catholic.

At first, all went well and uneventfully at the Center. Inevitably, the place felt the impact of the revolutionary sixties. Social activism had become so firmly established that Robert Hutchins found it difficult to justify the placid purposes of an operation that was designed at best to affect public policies very indirectly. More and more, the pressure to "do something" was felt throughout our remote, sylvan institution.

Actually, as editor of *The Center Magazine*, I was among the few whose duties included a conventional job. The magazine went far beyond our original hopes for it, its circulation soon topping the one hundred thousand mark. At the same time, I was personally employed by a new press service to write a weekly column which eventually reached millions of Catholics through twenty-odd diocesan papers. As with the *Commonweal* column, I was left free to wander all over the lot as a writer. Usually the column focused on contemporary secular themes, which I tried to integrate with traditional theological presuppositions.

I gave up the column (my own choice) after Pope Paul's disappointing encyclical on birth control in 1968. *Humanaé Vitae* did not of course claim to be infallible; it was the general Roman Catholic opinion that it was not, though it certainly qualified for reverential treatment since it bore the weight of the papacy. Like many other Catholics, I thought the encyclical deserved only contempt. I did not, however, join the dozens who took to the press or television to express their disagreement with the pope. Some of these same people also came to my office to say they had had it with the Church and were giving up on it. A few others, reverting to an old Catholic habit, expressed lofty indifference to the pope's statement, claiming they would carry on as usual, completely undisturbed by the latest (fallible) pronouncement from Rome.

I took the encyclical more seriously. I had been brought up to regard any papal statement with the utmost gravity and was not even tempted to denounce Paul personally in the column. I felt that he was quite serious and, though he chose to determine that the statement he made was not necessarily without error, he nevertheless expected that it would bind Roman Catholic consciences.

My conscience was at variance with the papal teachings, but according to Roman Catholic theology both before and after the Council, conscience took priority. I had always presumed, however, that the Church would enlighten my conscience. To put private judgment ahead of official Catholic teaching thoughtlessly—as some of my fellow religionists seemed to be doing—struck me as illogical. The pope may or may not choose to be infallible, but a solemn papal teaching on a matter of morals given to all men certainly had to be taken very seriously.

We were probably beyond the stage where the reaffirmed teaching on contraception would have very much practical effect in the United States. Nevertheless, I was quite disturbed that the most influential center of moral teaching in Christendom could be so dismally misleading.

I did not state my opinions in public at first. It still seemed very arrogant to contest papal teaching in public, especially on a matter of morals, though some of the youngest curates were doing precisely that. I fell back on the old Catholic teaching that an "obedient silence" was an appropriate reaction. But I could not in good conscience ignore the issue, so I wrote a final piece, giving fundamental dissent from the encyclical as my reason for discontinuing the column. I did not want to use the diocesan press to further undermine papal authority.

Immediately, I was solicited for a new column by the editors at my old stamping ground, *Commonweal*, and those at *The National Catholic Reporter*, both of which were independent Roman Catholic publications. I chose the *NCR*. For a couple of years I again wrote the kind of column I was used to. This, of course, was in addition to my work at the Center. Things were not going too well there, despite the growth of the magazine.

The basic argument seemed to focus on the issue of activism. The more recent members, especially the newly established junior fellows, were all for *doing* something. They took a dim view of the ripe age of the average fellow as a sure sign that the Center had lost touch with the youth-oriented 1960s. On the contrary, those who sided with Hutchins—ironically a former "boy wonder"—held that the trouble with freshmen-led movements was that their leaders soon became sophomores.

The speakers at the Center were frequently outstanding participants in the social ferment that characterized the decade—Daniel Berrigan, Michael Rossman, Tom Hayden, *et al.* I especially remember a series of guests who represented the "radical caucus" in this or that academic society.

The new activism suited Ping Ferry exactly. He was always eager for involvement in public affairs and never really satisfied with the complacent "study" the Center formally limited itself to. John Seeley, the dean, was seemingly quite uncritical of any activity involving youth. Bishop Pike pursued "Christian relevance" doggedly. Others had grown used to the permissive ambience of the Center and did not seem very concerned about its daily life. They came and went as they pleased.

After almost a decade, there was still no written constitution. Robert Hutchins presided without challenge, and Ashmore (no longer editor of the *Encyclopaedia Britannica*) had become his very subservient executive vice-president. Stormy staff meetings, later remembered with supreme distaste, were held every week. The role of the Center, rationally conceived, was heatedly debated at those meetings, with the issues usually settled in Hutchins' favor.

At one meeting, the president announced abruptly that the Center needed reorganization and more democraticization. There was general agreement that some of the present fellows were superfluous. But how to eliminate them? If there were a general election, then the very fellows who were deemed incapable of serving would have a strong voice in staffing the more intellectual Center of the future. If the decision was made by Hutchins alone, dictatorship would be charged.

Actually a suggestion of mine ultimately carried the day. I proposed that Hutchins (who was on everyone's list) be accepted as the first senior fellow. Hutchins then would pick a second person; the second, a third; and the third, a fourth—until there was no additional senior fellow chosen. Hutchins presented this plan to the group. All present agreed that it was not perfect, but as fair a method as had been devised. They decided to follow it. Each of us was sure that he would be among the few chosen by his peers. Of the senior staff only one fellow, John Wilkinson, cautiously pointed out that the second man chosen would, to a great extent, influence the remaining choices. He turned out to be right.

Ping Ferry was in Europe on vacation at the time, so had no responsibility for the decisions. But the others, even the visiting fellows (with one exception), agreed to the plan. The next week the fatal elections were held. Each new member added to the chosen group meant that all those remaining were gone over again as potential senior fellows, who—Hutchins assured everyone—would henceforth have complete charge of the Center's program.

In all, six fellows were chosen this way, including myself. There were, then, a number of leftovers. They were magnificently recompensed monetarily for past service with the Center, but almost all were embittered over this rejection by former confrères. Most of the leftovers were easily persuaded that they had been ill-judged by persons who were their actual intellectual inferiors. Strong feelings were engendered against the victorious "cabal," as the survivors were quickly branded. Ping Ferry, one of the veterans who lost, actually brought his case against the Center to civil court. Of course, the Center itself received widespread bad publicity because of the mass dismissals.

Bishop Pike was not elected a senior fellow, but he remained extraordinarily affable throughout. He soon took off for Israel with his young wife Diane to visit the Holy Land in preparation for a book he had agreed to write on the "historic Jesus." It was less than three months after he was let go by the Center that he died dramatically in the same Jerusalem desert Christ had retired to in order to pray.

It was freely predicted that with so many of the stellar figures gone, the program of the Center was doomed. The national press did little to change that impression. At the Center itself, some of those who remained entertained exaggerated ideas of the intellectual possibilities in a new start. Actually, it worked out that there were no very significant changes in the program. President Hutchins scrupulously kept his word about turning over the authority for the academic side of the Center to the new senior fellows, and regular meetings were held for collegial discussion of such matters.

The group was certainly not the "cabal" that it had been charged with being. Actually there was no special affinity among the senior fellows. Indeed, some were personally much closer to those who had left the Center then to their current colleagues. There was more international activity than previously and a stronger emphasis on involving established academicians like Mircea Eliade and Gunnar Myrdal in the program. The former humanistic emphasis was replaced by technology and science. In the interests of the Center, I attended meetings in Israel, the Austrian Alps, Malta, and in Cuernavaca, as well as gatherings throughout the United States. These meetings were accurately satirized in Arthur Koestler's *The Call Girls*.

The Center Magazine remained my special responsibility. As editor, I was limited to publishing material discussed at the table or written by persons formally affiliated with the institution. When I agreed to take the job, I had insisted on editorial independence within these limits. That editorial privilege—the only arrangement I found conceivable—was consistently honored by other senior fellows, with only occasional grumbling.

While the chores of being an editor of *The Center Magazine* and a senior fellow became routinized, my younger children were going through high school and college—Amherst, St. John's (Santa Fe), San Francisco State, the University of California, and Oberlin. Our family life was following the predictable, middle-class pattern.

Of course, the sixties were a particularly hard time for raising a family of teen-age children. Moral values were changing fast; old patterns of behavior no longer held. We had always been comparatively "easy" parents, without overdoing the permissiveness. Though there were the inevitable blow-ups between strong-minded children of one generation and protective parents of another, there was nevertheless basic harmony in the family. One by one the children left home for school, marriage, or personal adventure. We found ourselves, for the first time in more than a quarter of a century of marriage, childless in a big house.

I continued to do free-lance writing and even published two books: one based on the *Encyclopaedia* article, *Religion in a Secular Age*, and the other for a series marking the nation's bicentennial, *Catholic America*, a kind of historical portrait of Roman Catholicism in the United States.

Like many other persons of my way of thought, I was outraged by the Vietnam war, which I had opposed from the beginning. Night after night on the televised news, the "body count" of the day led me to be thankful that none of our sons was in the service—yet. However, the draft hung over us like the sword of Damocles. If anyone asked me to sign a petition, write an antiwar article, or march in a peace parade, I was all too ready to do so.

At the invitation of Clergy And Laity Concerned About Vietnam, I accompanied a group on a visit to American deserters in Paris and Stockholm. The idea was to unearth their spiritual needs and publicize their fate. The investigating group represented all faiths and none, and the age of the visiting delegates ranged over decades.

My other major involvement in antiwar activity brought me back to political life. Theodora and I happened to be in Washington in the fall of 1967 visiting our eldest son Terence, who was establishing his family in the D.C. area. As usual, I phoned my friend, Senator Eugene J. McCarthy. Theodora was listening to the Huntley-Brinkley news on NBC. While on the phone with the senator, I could hear the name "McCarthy" in the background.

Gene told me that on that very day he had formally announced his candidacy for the Democratic nomination, despite the fact that President Johnson was considered a shoo-in for renomination. He explained that his move was motivated by a strong moral antipathy to Johnson's Vietnam policies.

I was excited by the prospect of someone within the system trying to unseat Johnson, and I joined the campaign then and there. Later that evening, we had dinner with the McCarthys in a Georgetown restaurant. Theodora and I were aghast that even in Washington the senator went unrecognized. Still later I wrote to our son Chris, then a sophomore at Amherst, urging him to get his classmates—among whom was David Eisenhower—to support McCarthy's candidacy.

I do not think I contributed a great deal to McCarthy's strategy but I was with him during the lonely days in New Hampshire. I also accompanied McCarthy to Wisconsin, Indiana, Kentucky, and California.

I was much older than the average campaign worker, but that did not seem to matter greatly. Later one night, in an Indianapolis restaurant, my path crossed with Robert Kennedy's—the chief threat to the McCarthy candidacy, his surprising announcement after Gene's upset in New Hampshire had taken the bloom off the original enthusiasm generated by that victory.

This time Kennedy and I were on opposite sides in a political contest. But he was very cordial and recalled our earlier campaign in his brother's race. I remained loyal to McCarthy 'til the end, but would not have deemed it a great tragedy if Kennedy had taken the big prize, as he might well have had the assassin's bullet misfired.

McCarthy was genial enough, but somewhat difficult to work with. For one thing, his thinking was ultra-Thomistic and, therefore, he spoke in a language that many of his young liberal followers did not understand. He was too intellectually sophisticated to give much heed to their repetition of the facile slogans of the day, and much too self-conscious to make the basically empty liberal gestures that were endearing Robert Kennedy to millions.

McCarthy is a very private, proud man and these qualities did not endear him to some of his own followers. He found it excrutiatingly hard to make the most routine request or to say a simple thank you. He was acerbic in his comments on just about everyone, speaking of obvious faults and failures and generally passing over virtues. His speech was full of verbal gymnastics—paradox, puns, and attention-getting metaphors—but he was sparing in the use of his verbal gifts.

At times McCarthy's lassitude, despite the surrounding enthusiasm he engendered, was marked enough to indicate a basic indifference to the whole campaign effort. It seemed that every time the young McCarthy workers were about to apotheosize him, he would say something or do something to painfully remind them of his weaknesses.

His seeming arrogance and indolence, I have always thought, is really based on shyness and unusual reticence. He is a man of reverence, profound political conviction, and a deep-seated concern for social equity. He was one of the first members of Congress to espouse the cause of black people in America—when it took real courage to do so. The black community, however, never gave him the enthusiastic response lavished on the more outgoing Robert F. Kennedy.

Another outstanding quality of his is moral courage. It was particularly valuable at a time when leaders in Washington were often privately decrying a slaughter that they publicly supported. Gene McCarthy stood up at that time, when opposition in the Senate was an unpopular pose to take. His moral opposition to the war never wavered.

As time went on, his lacklustre campaign developed into the usual hoopla welcome at airports and screaming mobs in city auditoriums. McCarthy's victories began to add up. The response to his lonely challenge became so obvious that, in March, Lyndon Johnson announced his retirement.

Of course, despite its huge significance as a youth movement, McCarthy was beaten in California. Robert Kennedy, the victor, was slain. The ultimate Democratic candidate turned out to be the affable, conventional Hubert H. Humphrey, who almost defeated Richard M. Nixon.

I am not sure now that Eugene McCarthy would have made a good President, but my reservations do not bear at all on his intellectual qualifications. In fact, I still consider him a genius, of sorts. He is also one of the most far-sighted Americans to ever enter politics. He is about a decade ahead of his time; too far ahead, in any case, to be readily comprehended by the average voter.

REFLECTION SEVEN

During this period, the revolution in the Roman Catholic Church accelerated. I found, however, that I was becoming more Episcopalian than Roman. I now openly took the Anglican view of valid orders, for instance. In time, I had no hesitation whatsoever about receiving Holy Communion from the hands of an Episcopal cleric. The reason for the change, it finally dawned on me, was simple. There actually was no Episcoal Church in the sense of a theologically produced body within Christianity. There was, to be sure, an Anglican communion of Churches, in which was included the Protestant (in the sense of non-Roman) Episcopal Church of the United States, the original Church of England, the Church of Ireland, the Iglesa Episcopal do Brasil, the Church of the Province of Kenya, as well as many other individual Christian bodies. But there were no "Episcopal" sacraments, no "Episcopal" ministry, no "Episcopal" theology. There was no magic moment in which a Christian believer became an Episcopalian, but a moment when one simply recognized that one was a baptized Christian who practiced the faith in the Anglican mode.

I would not have to change any basic Christian belief in order to be a member of the Episcopal Church —there would be no conversion, no apostasy. I would not be required to sign any loyalty oaths in order to qualify to receive the Christian sacraments the Church offered.

Of course, there were some denials of Roman teaching that I would make as not arising from the Scriptures, were I to become an Anglican. I could no longer, for instance, declare that the pope and the Roman Catholic hierarchy could do much more than confer the absolution of sins that Christ had promised to all who accepted him, as recorded in Holy Scripture. The divine favor, I finally concluded, was simply not the rag doll of the hierarchy. For instance, I no longer held that they could confer indulgences at will, or "infallibly" decree truths which were derived "developmentally" from the original deposit of faith–in accordance with their own interpretation of "development." I no longer believed that every Christian on earth was subject to their interpretation of what was essential for the conferring of Christ's sacraments. I questioned the ample scope they gave the Christian tradition in order to justify later dogmas.

I no longer believed they could put strings on or withhold a natural right such as marriage—from priests and bishops, for instance—for pragmatic reasons. I no longer believed that there was a bona fide magisterium that might, even in the interests of protecting the "little ones," forbid scholarly scriptural studies or determine what books may or may not be read by the faithful. The Roman Church, now moving in that direction itself, seemed partially to agree.

Of course, for most people, having reached this conclusion, the move to the Episcopal Church would have been no more than a matter of going to Episcopal services, receiving the sacraments there, and henceforth identifying oneself as Anglican to family and friends. My case was somewhat different. I was publicly known as a Roman Catholic. I had been free with my opinions in that communion for years. There was every reason for readers to presume that, however controversial my political opinions, my orthodoxy (from Rome's point of view) was uncompromising. I had to announce publicly that my notion of what a Christian was, had changed somewhat. I had to say I wanted to be identified with that body of believers who are known in this country as Episcopalians. I owed that much frankness to the people who had, through the years, trusted my sincerity even when they did not agree with my opinions.

One evening when the Crowthers were visiting, I surprised the bishop by asking him to arrange for my formal reception into the Episcopal Church. He did not especially encourage me, though he placed no obstacles in the way either. He merely suggested that I think over the decision, weighing all factors. I continued to read Cardinal Newman and other divines who had once faced the same choice and had turned in the opposite direction.

I did as Crowther advised for the next several weeks, privately dwelling in a kind of ecumenical twilight zone. Reading Cardinal Newman's luminous prose, I tried to give him the benefit of every argument. Newman's urbane apologetics, however, struck me as hopelessly outdated, after De Ecclesia. *In Rome I had heard that John Henry Newman had more influence on the Council than any other theologian. I wondered now how long it had been since they had read anything by the English prelate.*

One thing was clear to me. Personalities had nothing to do with my final decision. Episcopalians and Roman Catholics, I could see at first hand, were about equal in both virtue and vice, though their social style might vary radically. There were conservatives and radicals in both Churches. Malcolm Boyd and Daniel Berrigan, like Gommar de Pauw and the editors of the Anglican Digest, *were not in competition with each other. I was not expecting to go from a sinful Church to one without stain. One thing I could not hope escape in any of the Churches was sin.*

I was seeking to come as close as I could get to the one, holy, Catholic, and apostolic Church that Christ seemed to envision. I thought I had finally found it in the Episcopal Church. Anglicanism existed within the Christian Church; perhaps with some undue pride, but without theological excrescence, addition, or the kind of "development" I now regarded as a largely misleading description of venerable old myths which had been added to the Christian dogmatic inheritance.

As a baptized Christian, I did not feel that I had been "converted" or that I would "apostasize" in changing denominational affiliation. What was I "converted" to, if I still accepted the Bible, the Church's essential tradition, and its sacraments? If I were to remain a Christian—a purified one, perhaps—how could I be called an apostate?

Conversion . . . apostate . . . heretic. These words were harsh. I do not say they did not sting when they were later used about me. But most of all they indicated how deeply the old defensive theology of the "one true Church," which had dominated Roman Catholicism from Trent until Vatican II, still penetrated those who used them.

CHAPTER XIII

The Episcopal Church

I WAS formally received into the Episcopal Church in September, 1973, by Bishop Crowther at Mount Calvary Retreat, a remote Anglican monastery of the Order of the Holy Cross in the mountains near Santa Barbara.

Theodora and our daughter Joan, attended the regular monastic Mass with me. In the middle of the familiar Eucharist, Bishop Crowther accepted my pledge of obedience to the Episcopal ordinary of California. I stated that I accepted the Episcopal body as a part of Christ's Holy Catholic Church. I was not asked to forswear anything that had been sacramentalized in the past or to renounce any peculiarly Roman Catholic belief.

When it was over, before nine in the morning, I went to work a happy man. I felt relieved because I realized that never again could it be presumed that I believed certain dogmas that I wordlessly denied and certain others that I was totally indifferent to. I could deny the infallibility of ecclesiastical councils and the divine supremacy of the Bishop of Rome. I no longer professed to believe that the full Christian truth was entrusted solely to a small percentage of Christians, but that we all saw through a glass, darkly. My belief, now formal, was that all Christians were in possession of the basic Christian truths through the Scriptures; the residue of the remaining theological lore was interesting but did not ultimately matter. I was naturally pleased to be free of the moral discipline and regulations imposed in the name of Jesus Christ's "one true Church" by the Roman Curia.

The liturgy of the new Church was only slightly different from

122

what I had known. Most of the peculiarities of Roman Catholic worship could now be practiced if I found them devotional, or ignored if I found them offensive. I no longer felt any guilt because I found that saying the rosary was a bore and Benediction of the Blessed Sacrament a stately but senseless exercise. There are Anglicans who practice both, of course, but there are others who feel free to march out of the church when they begin. (Of course there is no dogmatic character given to these practices in the Roman communion either; but they are highly valued "pious practices" and enjoy official commendation. To reject them out of hand would have required more daring than I had.)

The advantage in staying where I was would have been that I would not have had to turn my back on the religio-ethnic community in which I was reared and in which I had enjoyed a certain prestige. As I grew older, and as ancient controversies died out, that position might have mellowed into something like honor and respect. In late middle age, I was going into an alien community, one historically hostile to my forefathers, generally identified in America with a class into which I was not born. I was not leaving Roman Catholicism by mindless attrition, as so many were in those days, but by liturgized decision.

To make things worse, I felt no bitter sentiments toward the Church I was leaving. I knew that the antidemocratic charges made against American Catholics were baseless and that Catholics in this country were superbly acceptable in their American sentiments. They were, in fact, largely indifferent to the ancient canard that they had to choose between two masters: the pope and Uncle Sam. I did not personally feel that I was separating myself from the "ideal" Church that really already united Anglican and Roman Catholic. I knew that this idea was, sadly, not a present reality but only a hope for the future and that it probably would not be actualized in my lifetime.

If I were angry with the priests or hierarchy of Rome, if I had been seriously "hurt" by them (as one monk friend later suggested), or if I were without hope for Roman Catholicism, there might then be extenuating circumstances for my so-called "apostasty"; but there was no such evidence in my case.

After the ceremony at Mount Calvary, I informed the *National Catholic Reporter* by letter of what I had done. In the letter to the *NCR*, I did not elaborate on why I had left the Church of my birth for, of all things, Anglicanism. Theodora and I then went immediately to Mexico to remain incommunicado when the *Reporter* published the story on its front page. The item was thereafter taken up by the news services and *The New York Times*.

Reactions to my change of Churches were revealing. Most friends—Roman Catholic, Anglican, Protestant, Jewish, and agnostic—did not really care. Predictably, I received a small number of letters from old-style conservative Catholics, promising their prayers for my return to true Christianity. The outgoing Presiding Bishop of the Episcopal Church, John Hines, sent me a welcoming telegram. Some of the few Anglican divines I knew personally sent words of encouragement, with no hint of religious triumphalism. I received a few letters from Roman Catholics who were holding on for dear life, wondering whether they might also come to accept Anglicanism as valid Christianity. (I did not encourage them to change.) A prominent Roman Catholic priest inaccurately used my case as an example of the once-ardent Catholic who found the *aggiornamento* so disappointingly slow that he decided to move elsewhere and avoid the incessant internal turmoil in the Roman Church.

A few Catholics affected boredom and elaborate indifference to the case. Dan Herr, the lay publisher of *The Critic*, wrote that it was time the "John Cogleys of this world stop taking themselves so damn seriously and spare the rest of us their pompous pronouncements." I had tried to avoid pomposity in my announcement in *The National Catholic Reporter*, but I suppose the very fact that I wrote such a letter was an indication that Mr. Herr had hit pay dirt.

Later, the editor of *The New York Times'* Op Ed page requested a short article about my journey from Rome to Canterbury, which I obligingly and foolishly honored. I had hoped at the time that the article might inform some of my friends who did not keep up with *The Nation Catholic Reporter* about the big change in my life. The article seemed to enrage Andrew Greeley. He described its author in a subsequent column, not only as a clever "apostate," but as a "vain little man with an exaggerated notion of his own importance." The extent of my "vanity and shallowness," I took it, was clearly displayed to him in the *Times* piece. All in all, "we might be well rid of him," Father Greeley concluded.

It seems to me that the Churches must be united or disappear from the modern world. I now believe that the Anglican branch of the Church gives the best example for that future united Christian Church. One reason for this is the very antiquity of the Anglican communion. There were British bishops at the Council of Arles in the fourth century. Another reason is the present democratic structure which the Episcopal Church somehow manages to combine with episcopacy. Third, its freedom of theological investigation pays off in the long run; just as it did decades ago when the Church, contradicting an earlier position, gave its approval of birth control. I feel confident that it will continue in this tradition when it authorizes the ordination of women to the priesthood. Fourth, there is the Anglican insistence that every doctrine must be "proved" by the Scriptures before it may be enforced as a point of belief. The only Anglican certainty is its devotion to the Savior and his teachings; its only *Summa Theologica* is the Bible itself.

For that reason it has never excluded other Christian denominations from the Church of Christ, even Roman Catholics during a period when feelings against Rome were exacerbated by political loyalties. Today, one finds a carving of John Henry Newman in the elaborate pulpit of St. Thomas Episcopal Church in Manhattan and a window commemorating the beloved pontiff, John XXIII, in Grace Cathedral in San Francisco, where the Jesuit theologian Karl Rahner is also depicted in stained glass.

This kind of ecumenical gesture, forgetting bitter past history, has a tremendous appeal. I am convinced that I have found the right Church for me when I see the excellent relations the Episcopal Church enjoys with Greek Orthodoxy and Protestanism in general.

I used to hope that the Roman Catholic Church would take the lead in ecumenical endeavors. But that hope was lost some time after Vatican II. The will is there, of course; most Roman Catholics are ready for a greater communion of Churches. But I am afraid that the uncompromising Roman insistence on the God-given primacy of the pope and the residuum of the "one true Church" idea will stand as a blockade to Christian unity, at least for my lifetime.

Right now, everything concerned with ecclesiastical structure and doctrinal loyalty—the infallibility of the pope, the exact number of sacraments, the "validity" of Holy Orders, Baptism by immersion, for example—seems much more important to many churchpeople than Christian unity. This is how things will surely remain for a time.

I hope that the Episcopal Church continues to give example. But I certainly do not wish to convert any other Christian to Anglicanism. I only hope that belief in Christ remains a liberating rather than a confining fact of life for everyone. It is Jesus Christ who must remain the center of Christian lives; it was his cause that all the Churches were meant to serve, rather than impede. Christianity was supposed to bring mankind to unity.

L'envoi

ON June 11, 1974, during a conference at the Center for the Study of Democratic Institutions on the role of religion in contemporary life, which I was co-chairing with Professor Jerald Bruer of the University of Chicago, I was tried in my new ecclesiastical allegiance: I had a serious cerebral stroke. For the next month, I was very ill at the Cottage Hospital in Santa Barbara. The following month I spent at a stroke victims' rehabilitation center, where I was retrained to take up ordinary life.

I finally returned to the Center. But it was clear after some months that I could not keep up with the work and would henceforth be a burden to those in charge. Consequently, I resigned my post as editor of *The Center Magazine* and was appointed an unpaid associate. I spent the next year recovering at home and writing this book.

After some months, I applied to the Episcopal Diocese of California for ordination to the priesthood in the "one, Holy, Catholic, and Apostolic Church," and I was accepted.

I am now an Episcopal cleric. Coming so late in life, mine will necessarily be a short ministry; my prayer is that it will be a fruitful one.

My whole life, as I see it now, has led up to this move. What had gone before seems no more than a proper preface for what appears to lie ahead, if God preserves me for a while.